OLD PERITHIA

ΠΑΛΙΑ ΠΕΡΙΘΕΙΑ

MERCHANT'S HOUSE PUBLISHING

www.old-perithia.com

Old Perithia 49081 Corfu Greece

CONTENTS

ΠΕΡΙΕΧΟΜΕΝΑ

WELCOME TO OLD PERITHIA

ΚΑΛΩΣΗΛΘΑΤΕ ΣΤΗΝ ΠΑΛΙΑ ΠΕΡΙΘΕΙΑ

Welcome to Old Perithia. A 14th century village of Venetian architecture, built entirely by hand. This historic village is encircled by eight beautiful churches and can be found just below the highest mountain in Corfu, at the foot of Mount Pantokrator (The Almighty). Distinctive and picturesque, Old Perithia is a protected heritage site and designated as 'an area of outstanding natural beauty'.

"Old Perithia - A wonderful marriage between history, architecture and nature."

"Παλιά Περίθεια - Ένα Θαυμαστό Πάντρεμα Ιστορίας, Αρχιτεκτονικής και Φύσης."

AN INTRODUCTION FROM THE PUBLISHER

ΕΙΣΑΓΩΓΙΚΟ ΣΗΜΕΙΩΜΑ ΤΟΥ ΕΚΔΟΤΗ

In the following pages, we will guide you around **Old Perithia** and reveal the history that surrounds this ancient settlement, along with its mystery, myth and even its miracles.

Some things remain unknown about the village as the stories have been picked over so many times and embroidered in so many places. However, every surviving account of the story of Old Perithia confirms that it is the oldest settlement on the island of Corfu, dating back to 1347 and beyond.

From our extensive research and time spent here, we hope to provide as accurate a description as possible, not to rewrite history, but to uncover it.

To this end, each new edition will include new discoveries about this unique mountain village and its inhabitants.

Throughout the rest of the guide, we will refer to the village by its 'modern name', **Old Perithia,** although we will explain the origins of the name in more detail later.

However, it is not our words or pictures that we hope will most stimulate your five (or possibly six) senses, but the village itself and the wild beauty that surrounds it.

Our purpose is to guide you whilst you are here, and, when you have left, we hope that this guide will bring back wonderful memories of Old Perithia, until you return some day in the future, by yourselves, with friends, or with future generations.

Tighten your shoelaces because there is no more enjoyable way to explore Old Perithia than to follow the paths around the village.

Ο πιο ευχάριστος τρόπος για να ανακαλύψετε την Παλιά Περίθεια είναι να ακολουθήσετε τα μονοπάτια γύρω από το χωριό.

Θερμές ευχαριστίες προς τους κατοίκους της Παλιάς και Νέας Περίθειας για τη βοήθεια και υποστήριξή σας. Παρακαλούμε επικοινωνήστε μαζί μας εάν έχετε να προτείνετε περισσότερες πληροφορίες ή διορθώσεις. Θέλουμε να ακούσουμε τα σχόλιά σας για την επόμενη έκδοση του οδηγού.

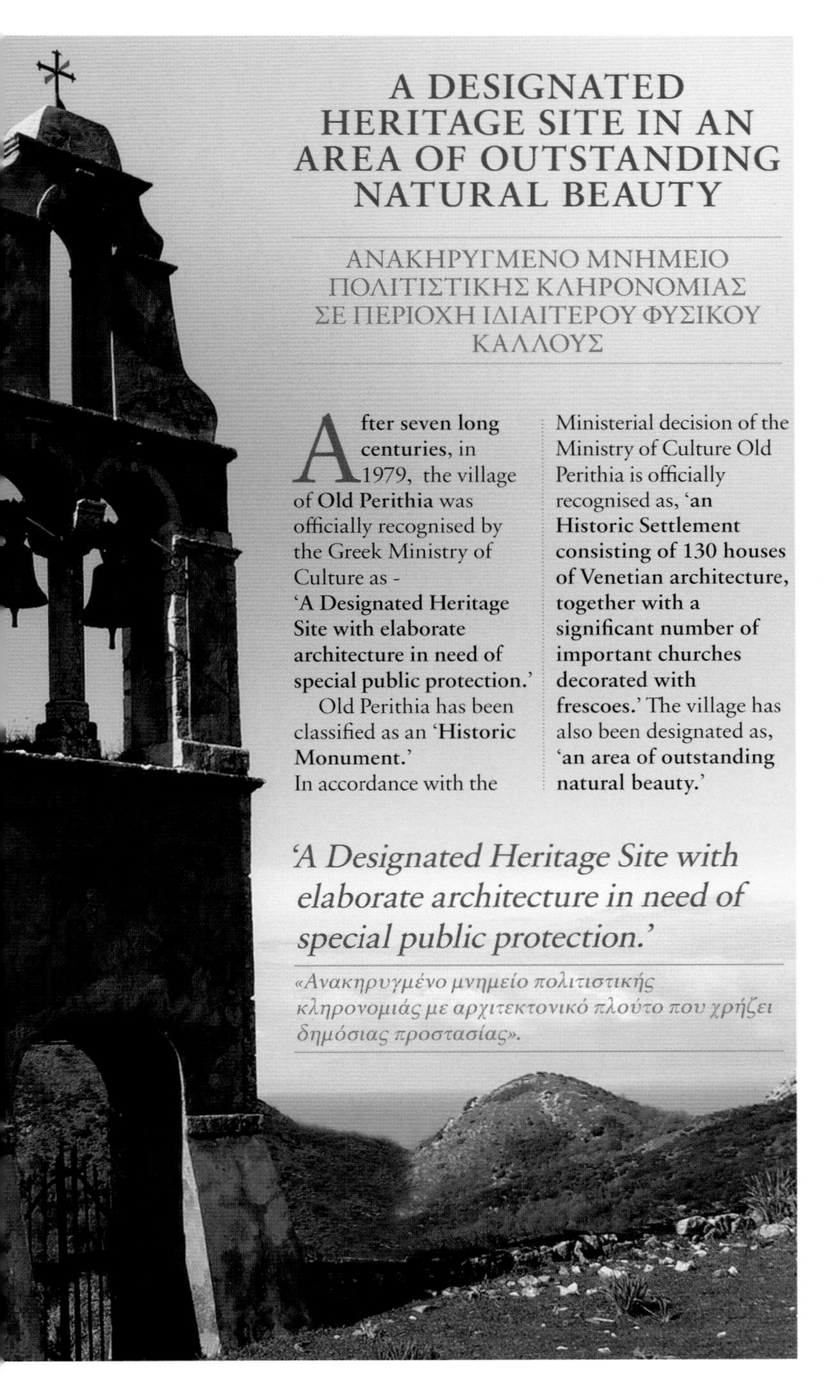

A DESIGNATED HERITAGE SITE IN AN AREA OF OUTSTANDING NATURAL BEAUTY

ΑΝΑΚΗΡΥΓΜΕΝΟ ΜΝΗΜΕΙΟ ΠΟΛΙΤΙΣΤΙΚΗΣ ΚΛΗΡΟΝΟΜΙΑΣ ΣΕ ΠΕΡΙΟΧΗ ΙΔΙΑΙΤΕΡΟΥ ΦΥΣΙΚΟΥ ΚΑΛΛΟΥΣ

After seven long centuries, in 1979, the village of **Old Perithia** was officially recognised by the Greek Ministry of Culture as - **'A Designated Heritage Site with elaborate architecture in need of special public protection.'**

Old Perithia has been classified as an **'Historic Monument.'**
In accordance with the Ministerial decision of the Ministry of Culture Old Perithia is officially recognised as, **'an Historic Settlement consisting of 130 houses of Venetian architecture, together with a significant number of important churches decorated with frescoes.'** The village has also been designated as, **'an area of outstanding natural beauty.'**

'A Designated Heritage Site with elaborate architecture in need of special public protection.'

«Ανακηρυγμένο μνημείο πολιτιστικής κληρονομιάς με αρχιτεκτονικό πλούτο που χρήζει δημόσιας προστασίας».

Photograph: Courtesy of Mihalis Kokkalis

 OLD PERITHIA

THE ORIGINS AND A BRIEF HISTORY OF THE OLD VILLAGE

ΠΡΟΕΛΕΥΣΗ ΚΑΙ ΣΥΝΤΟΜΗ ΙΣΤΟΡΙΑ ΤΟΥ ΠΑΛΙΟΥ ΧΩΡΙΟΥ

IN GREEK - Ano (Upper) or Palia (Old) Peritheia - Παλιά Περίθεια
ENGLISH - Old Perithia

Hidden in the mountains, Old Perithia, with its sun-drenched limestone ruins glowing white, pink and ochre, is one of the most historic and beautiful villages to be found on the island of Corfu.

OLD PERITHIA AN INFORMAL INTRODUCTION

ΕΙΣΑΓΩΓΗ ΣΤΗΝ ΠΑΛΙΑ ΠΕΡΙΘΕΙΑ

There are many stories about the earliest origins of Old Perithia, but of all of these, one in particular stands out.

Around 300-350BC there was a coastal village around Acharavi with a population of approximately 2,500 people. Following an earthquake, a tidal wave swept the coast killing the majority of the community and leaving only 750 survivors.

The concerned and fearful families who remained sought a safer location and built eight new settlements in the mountains (all of which exist to this day) one of which was called Perithia.

Many centuries later, with the constant threat of pirate attacks on the island, another village was built higher up. That village was Upper Perithia (Ano Perithia) which explains the Old, and New, Perithia of today. An observation point (vigla) was built in Old Perithia looking out to sea.

The families split their time between the summer, in Old Perithia (tending their vineyards, fruit trees, crops and livestock), and the winter when they returned to their settlements farther down.

There are various versions about the origin of the name Perithia.

Υπάρχουν πολλές εκδοχές για την προέλευση του ονόματος Περίθεια.

The first sign (or proof) of Old Perithia's existence was found on a parchment dating back to 1347 and signed by Monk Anthimos of Perithia. However, it has been established that the village is almost certainly more ancient than this.

Many believe the name derives from a combination of peri and theia (literally 'surrounded by The Holy'). This refers to the numerous churches in the village and the nearby monastery of Pantokrator (Monastery of The Almighty) built in 1347 with the help of the Perithiotes (or Perithians, the inhabitants of Perithia).

Another hypothesis is the combination of peri and thea (meaning 'all seeing') due to its strategic position and views of the sea, but it is also surrounded by mountains.

Others attribute the name to the ancient Nymphs who, according to Isyhios, were called 'Pirithoi'. But in ancient times there were other Nymphs too. In Homer's Odyssey, he wrote of **"Nymphs, who haunt the steep hilltops, the springs of rivers, and the grassy meadows."**

Whilst there is a spring in Old Perithia, rivers and natural springs are not in abundance unlike the aptly named village of 'Nymphes', one of the largest villages in the Municipality of Thinali, where there are many springs and waterfalls. This suggests that neither the Pirithoi nor Homer's reference in the Odyssey relate in any way to Old Perithia. Nevertheless, in summary, the most popular and probable theory is that the name derives from the words 'peri theia' (surrounded by The Holy) because the village is, **at the foot of The Almighty** (Mount Pantokrator) and **surrounded by eight churches.**

Old Perithia is therefore a village 'Surrounded by The Almighty.'

'Περικυκλωμένη από τον Παντοκράτορα.'

The Grand Entrance Arch to Skordilis Mansion (The Old School) -
Η μεγάλη αψίδα στην είσοδο του αρχοντικού Σκορδίλη (Το παλιό σχολείο)

INVISIBLE FROM THE SEA - THE PERFECT HIDING PLACE

ΑΘΕΑΤΗ ΑΠΟ ΤΗ ΘΑΛΑΣΣΑ - Η ΤΕΛΕΙΑ ΚΡΥΨΩΝΑ

LOOKING ACROSS THE VILLAGE AND MOUNTAINS TO THE SEA BEYOND

ΑΓΝΑΝΕΥΟΝΤΑΣ ΤΗ ΘΑΛΑΣΣΑ ΜΕΣΑ ΑΠΟ ΤΟ ΧΩΡΙΟ ΚΑΙ ΤΑ ΒΟΥΝΑ

Without any prior knowledge of the history of Old Perithia, the location at 420-480m (1400-1600 ft) up in the hills would make you wonder why its inhabitants originally chose such a rocky and inaccessible place to live. But, as you may have already read, or realised on your way into the village, it was actually the result of careful strategic planning.

During the 14th century, there were many attacks and pirate raids on Corfu. The settlements and homes that had been established in the foothills of the mountains were vulnerable.

Families sought refuge higher up and built second homes and communities where they could live and hide during the summer. **Out of sight - Out of mind.**

Old Perithia became the perfect location for a 'hidden' village where you could see…but not be seen.

The higher ground also offered a safe haven from the perils of both malaria and cholera that were prevalent at one time at Antinioti, and other coastal lakes and wetlands during the summer months.

The village is hidden from the sea, although the sea is clearly visible from the village.

Το χωριό είναι αθέατο από τη θάλασσα, όμως η θάλασσα φαίνεται καθαρά από το χωριό.

The Antinioti lagoon is situated along the coastline below the mountains.

As the threat of pirates, and latterly mosquitoes, subsided, many villagers who owned houses in both Old Perithia and the villages below (primarily New Perithia) moved back to their homes lower down the mountain and nearer to the coast. By the 1940's the village had gradually become more and more deserted. Then, with the dramatic rise in tourism in the 1960s and the supporting infrastructure, there seemed less and less reason to return.

But people have continued to be drawn to this beautiful village during the summer months for the cooler air, healthier lifestyle and to avoid the mosquitoes. Also, in winter, Old Perithia continues to draw families and friends from around the island (and adventurous tourists) who come to walk, explore or enjoy a leisurely traditional lunch at the bustling tavernas, all of which are invariably full practically every weekend.

The village was built in a north south direction with houses in two clusters, one each side of the village.

The layout, north and south with nothing in between, was designed to accommodate and channel any torrents of water, away from the houses and churches, during the winter and rainy season.

Families sought refuge higher up and built second homes and communities where they could hide during the summer. Out of sight - Out of mind.

Antinioti Lagoon

Λίμνη Αντινιώτη

Many centuries ago the Antinioti Lagoon, as with many low waters along coastlines, had become infested with mosquitoes. Combined with the stagnant water, this may have been the main cause of the malaria and cholera that, caused so many deaths in low lying villages in the area and, encouraged the movement of people to the mountain village of Old Perithia to avoid infection and disease. Hence its name, 'anti' or 'adis' - nioti (anti youth). It was also feared that it may have been Hades who was taking their young to the underworld, as was believed at the time.

Obviously that was many centuries ago. Antinioti has since become a natural wildlife habitat and is home to an array of flora, fauna, and many beautiful and rare orchids.

Photograph: Courtesy of Alkistis Prepis

In its heyday, the population of Old Perithia was around 1200 - 1500 people. There were approximately 130 houses, so this meant that many families lived together, often with up to ten people (including children) in a single house.

THE VILLAGE IS BUILT IN FOUR CLUSTERS

1. The Top (Kokkina)
2. The Centre (Foros)
3. After St. Spyridon (Pera Chorio)
4. The houses below the path leading back from St. Nikolaos of Petra to St. Iakovos, Persis (Karababa)

In its heyday, the population of Old Perithia was around 1200 - 1500 people. There were approximately 130 houses, so this meant that many families lived together, often with up to ten people (including children) in a single house.

Old Perithia was a self-sufficient community where nature could provide all that was needed. For certain other items, it meant a two-hour walk (and back) to other small settlements down below. It was a beautiful village in which the houses were built by hand, using local limestone and timber. These local materials were also in demand for building and masonry throughout the entire island.

Old Perithia was also a thriving community, the atmosphere warm and friendly, with neighbours often keeping each other company. They used to gather around, gossip and recount old tales, (often ghost stories!) and entertain each other both day and night. The 'social life' in the village was enhanced by the '**kafeneia**' (coffee shops). These were primarily meeting places, where you could get together for coffee, a glass of ouzo or a game of backgammon. They were frequently filled with the sound of music and alive with traditional dancing.

Kafeneia Καφενεία

Latterly, some of them became tavernas and shops relevant to the needs of the times, attracting many visitors from the villages nearby. Unfortunately, none of the original 'kafeneia' have survived the test of time.

The village mainly consists of a cluster of two-storey houses, typical of a post-Angevin tradition and Venetian architecture, with flat or narrow façades. A number of the properties are substantial and some of them retain morphological elements of the Renaissance, such as the noble Chirdaris and Skordilis mansions. Other 'notable' families of the village (whose houses can be seen as you walk around) are those of Sarakinos and Salvanos.

Sarakinos Mansions can be found behind Chirdaris Mansions along the path to the side. Salvanos' houses can be seen at the far end of the path to the side of Zoodochos Pigi.

The two main churches are those of St. Iakovos, Persis (now under the community of Loutses, along with another three) and St.

Nikolaos, Petra (once a female monastery), the only church built and owned by the village. The remaining three are 'family churches' and are all privately owned.

The island of Corfu offered security. Families came from many different locations, and those with wealth and influence became the nobles of Corfu. The nobles would travel by carriage from town to their village houses in the summer, but in winter the journey was often long and difficult. Old Perithia was one such example, with its village community encompassing noble houses along with many religious structures (churches and belfries) and the homes of its farmers and countrymen.

Corfu, for the eighty years prior to 1347, and for forty years after, had been under the kingdom of Sicily and Naples (the Angevin period 1267-1386), a fact that determined its social, economic and commercial life. This explains the early French-Italian influence on the architecture of both the island and the architectural style of Old Perithia, as it evolved throughout the second half of the 14th century.

Over the years, Corfu, under the influence of the Venetians, the French and the British, developed a culture of its own.

It was during the period of Venetian rule that the island saw an influx of men of learning and artists, as well as great families. Uprooted from their natural homes following the fall of Constantinople, Mystra, and a short while later Crete, they came to settle in Corfu. Together with officers of the Venetian state they acquired titles and land and so began the construction of many country houses, residences and 'manor houses' all built of stone.

These gave the island great character and examples (such as Old Perithia) can still be seen, despite their condition, projecting the authority and energy they enjoyed when first built.

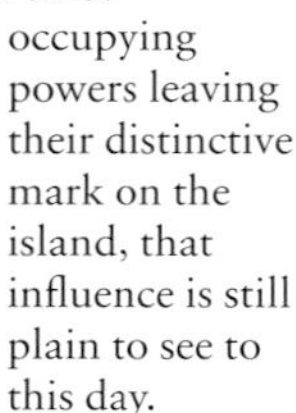

With all three occupying powers leaving their distinctive mark on the island, that influence is still plain to see to this day.

Some centuries ago, a thick forest blanketed the northern slopes of Mount Pantokrator. There were approximately 100,000 trees around the villages, including Old Perithia, and many magnificent trees can still be seen to this day. But, due to a number of complicated ownership issues and lack of any official protection or decree, many trees were cut down when the wood was needed for shipbuilding, houses or general building throughout the island.

All of the original stone houses were, unsurprisingly for the time and location, built by hand.

When you look around the village you'll notice some 'stone' houses and certain others with a flat and often painted, 'façade'. This had as much to do with wealth as the architectural style. Corfu and the mountains have a damp climate in winter, and a veneered façade was much preferred because it protected the houses against the effects of the weather. This was an additional cost that some villagers could not afford at that time, hence the mixture of the two styles.

The houses are predominantly on one or two floors, but there is one imposing three-storey house to be found in the village, although it has now practically fallen down.

There are a number of simple countrymen's >p.

Olive Trees

Ελιές

During their 400 year rule the Venetians encouraged the cultivation of olive trees. They rewarded large scale planting but barred the Corfiots from entering into commercial competition with Venice. Olive trees tended to grow best at anything up to 400m above sea level. At 420-480m the village of Old Perithia only had a few olive groves, but a substantial number of vineyards. It was a farming community and not such a prolific contributor to the now approximate three million olive trees on the island. Some old terraces can still be seen as you walk around the village, these were historically used for crops, such as corn and wheat.

"... rolling green-silver eiderdowns of giant olive trees, some reputedly over five hundred years old."

Extract from Birds, Beasts and other Relatives © Gerald Durrell 1969

Today visitors are rewarded with a fascinating glimpse into the way in which people used to live, as well as spectacular unspoiled mountain views, clean air, fresh water and the most extraordinary array of scents and smells.

Veranda - Botzo Βεράντα - Μπότζο

homes or labourer's cottages (single storey) with only a few details, as you'll see on the walk. Some of these had one side of the house built into the rock.

A number of these houses, in typical Venetian style, had engravings or blazons on the marble entrance doors and all of the two storey homes had external staircases. These lead to first floor verandas (botzos) with columns and were often decorated with potted plants.

A typical two-storey house often had a basement or ground floor (katoi) for storage or livestock, some with wooden containers for olive oil or barrels for wine.

Sometimes the ground floor was used as a shop or occasionally as stables. Above the ground (or basement floor), you could find a second, but rarely a third-storey, with bedrooms and/or additional living space.

In centuries past, villagers used a 'tap' for washing their hands and face. It was a small container hung on the wall and filled from the top with water. You then simply turned on the small tap (as illustrated).

Properties, throughout the island, had historically been just one or two storeys high. But from 1814, when the Ionian Islands were declared an independent state under the protection of Great Britain, the building and construction

A tap Βρύση

Loos in Medieval times?
Αποχωρητήρια της μεσαιωνικής εποχής

With the lack of a proper sewage system at the time, most people used a chamberpot and flung 'it' out the window or 'went for a walk'. Unless you had a substantial amount of land with your property, creating a deep hole in the rocky ground was an almost impossible and very expensive undertaking. In the noble houses there may possibly have been a plank of wood with a hole in it to sit on, or a chute that went to a cesspit or a small room outside.

World War One
Πρώτος Παγκόσμιος Πόλεμος

It is said that, during World War One, four German soldiers accidentally stumbled across the village. The villagers debated whether to let them live or 'get rid of them'. Fortunately they made the wise decision to let them wander freely around the village and, having found nothing of particular interest or benefit, they left the village in peace.

Throughout the war no German soldiers returned there and there were never any air raids on Old Perithia. If the villagers had decided to kill the soldiers, it may well have changed the course of history for Old Perithia...

in the towns literally took an 'upward turn' as more storeys were added to the houses to accommodate the growing economy. At the same time, as the locals acquired more land, they too began rebuilding or extending properties (as seen in Old Perithia). This is why you see many properties in the village with inscribed dates from around 1850.

The British remained until the Ionian islands were united with Greece in 1864 and Corfu regained its Greek identity. The centuries of foreign occupation came to an end. But, this also signalled the end of Corfu as the capital of the Ionian Islands.

With the passage of time, the community of Old Perithia gradually moved down towards the sea and to the village of '**New Perithia**', to seek their fortune from the growth of tourism and other local commerce. However, the families would still return to their original homes throughout the summer months, to avoid the mosquitoes, enjoy the clean mountain air, eat the healthy food and drink the local wine or fresh mountain spring water.

The village has a strange familiarity, as if the houses were 'old acquaintances'. It is a place of calm and serenity, offering its many visitors a safe haven from the frenetic pace of life.

Old Perithia effectively became deserted around the time of the World War Two.

Old Perithia in the municipality of Thinali (from the ancient Greek 'Para thin alos' - beside the sea) cannot fall prey to over development, alteration or expansion, because it is now designated as a protected heritage site and an area of outstanding natural beauty.

As the oldest remaining example of an ancient settlement in Corfu, the village of Old Perithia is unique to the island, and it is certainly considered as the most impressive 'original', and well preserved village that still exists to this day.

Over half a century after the village and its old farmsteads were all but deserted, some of the village properties, having patiently waited, are now being carefully restored. There are stunning views of the mountain scenery and sea beyond. Beautiful beaches and turquoise seas are just fifteen minutes drive away.

All this guarantees that the present and future inhabitants undoubtedly have the best of all worlds.

Finally, after seven long centuries of fighting for its own existence, Old Perithia is being lovingly restored and new life now breezes through this mountain village with every passing day.

> *To love a country is to love a people, but also its habits, customs and houses.*

Daniel Rozensztroch 'Greek Style'.

Photograph: Courtesy of Mihalis Kokkalis

A WALKING PICTURE TOUR OF THE OLD VILLAGE

ΠΕΡΙΠΑΤΗΤΙΚΗ ΞΕΝΑΓΗΣΗ ΣΤΟ ΠΑΛΙΟ ΧΩΡΙΟ ΜΕ ΦΩΤΟΓΡΑΦΙΕΣ

There's a '**fold out map**' on the inside back cover of the guide!
Simply follow the numbers

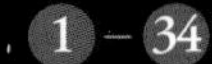

Χάρτης στο πίσω μέρος του εξώφυλλου.

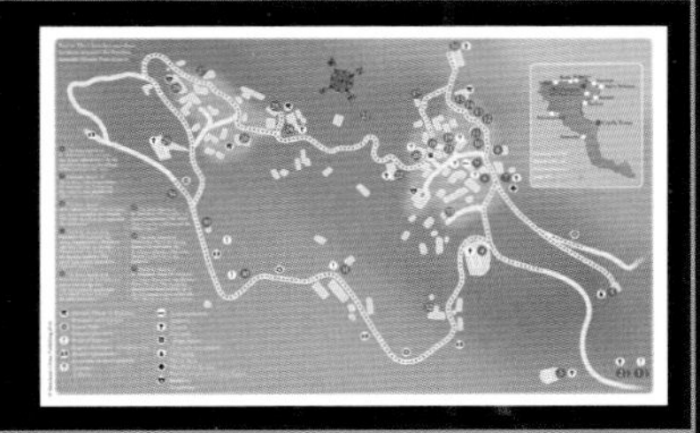

APPROACHING THE VILLAGE BY CAR

ΠΛΗΣΙΑΖΟΝΤΑΣ ΤΟΝ ΟΙΚΙΣΜΟ ΜΕ ΑΥΤΟΚΙΝΗΤΟ

Entrance to Old Perithia ① looking back - Είσοδος της Παλιάς Περίθειας

> *"You enter Greece as one might enter a dark crystal; the form of things becomes irregular, refracted. Other countries may offer you discoveries in manners or lore or landscape; Greece offers you something harder - the discovery of yourself."*

Extract from Prospero's Cell by Lawrence Durrell ©

The village is so **well hidden** that it cannot be seen from the road until you get quite close, so at first it may seem that it doesn't exist. But, as you get nearer, you will pass through the so-called **'entrance to the village'** ① where the road cuts between the rocks.

Moments later, **to your**

The Holy Church of St. Athanasios ② at the natural entrance to the village Η εκκλησία του Αγίου Αθανασίου στη φυσική είσοδο του χωριού

The Holy Church of Theotokos - The Virgin Mary ❸ Η εκκλησία της Υπεραγίας Θεοτόκου

right, down amidst the trees and bushes, you can see the first of the eight churches that surround the village. **The Holy Church of St. Athanasios ❷.** It is almost impossible to reach, except on foot, but good to spot on your way, coming in (or out) of Old Perithia, as it is the farthest church away from the village itself.

The density of trees that surround the church is a good illustration of the proliferation of trees (100,000) that once flourished in and around Old Perithia.

As you approach the start of the main village, be aware of straying goats or sheep that may appear from the mountains and undergrowth, and cross the road unexpectedly.

You will soon notice a track on your left-hand side with a small shrine at the bottom of the slope.

This track leads to the second church of the village, **The Holy Church of Theotokos - The Virgin Mary ❸, it's best to stop by here on your way out of the village.** Although the church is in a state of disrepair, it is equally fascinating and bewildering to see how it is being left to the ravages of both weather and time.

The Church of Theotokos (patiently awaiting some attention) is not clearly visible from the road, but if you walk up the track and glance through the entrance of the church on the right-hand side, you can still see the old pews and

The resident goatherd (and goats) crossing the road near the village Ο βοσκός του χωριού (με κατσίκες)

The Holy Church of St. Iakovos, Persis ❹ Άγιος Ιάκωβος, Πέρσης

candle holders beneath the dramatically collapsed roof. It is clear that the existing frescoes (templo) such as the wall painting of The Virgin Mary (now barely visible) and the marble works are all in need of meticulous conservation work.

To the exterior of the church, there is further evidence that the marble entrance and windows are in need of repair, as well as the bell tower, all of which have suffered serious damage with neglect, the passage of time, and subsequently the theft of both the marble and icons.

The Holy Church of St. Iakovos, Persis with its charming pink façade welcomes you to this beautiful place.

A couple of minutes later, when you arrive at the village your eye will be drawn to the iconic church and its dominant belfry that gazes gracefully across the whole of Old Perithia. This is the **Holy Church of St. Iakovos, Persis** ❹.

It is as if the church with its charming pink façade welcomes you to this beautiful place, its belfry appears to stand as a loyal guardian of the homes and people of Old Perithia, the oldest village of Corfu.

Parking Πάρκινγκ

Please park carefully and considerately, as far back from the main village as possible, to help retain the natural view of the church, historic houses and restored taverna as you enter the village. Also, the local goatherd and his wife often need to cross the road and have access in and out of the village (with their goats or sheep), so please don't block the roads and pathways.

THE WALKING TOUR INTRODUCTION

ΠΕΡΙΠΑΤΗΤΙΚΗ ΞΕΝΑΓΗΣΗ - ΕΙΣΑΓΩΓΗ

It is here that our circular walk around Old Perithia begins, so, a few notes before you set off.

Using the map (on the inside back cover), the tour will take you full circle around the village and back to the pink church of St. Iakovos, Persis ❹. The walk is approximately 2km and designed to take about an hour or so, depending on your temptation to stop along the way. Although good footwear is recommended, the walk is not strenuous and you are never far from the starting point. **Please take special care if you are entering old buildings, as you do so entirely at your own risk.**

We have added **pictures and information** at **key points of interest** along the way, **together with additional photos to guide you around the village.**

SO, LET'S BEGIN...

ΑΣ ΑΡΧΙΣΟΥΜΕ ΛΟΙΠΟΝ...

THE RECOMMENDED TOUR

Η ΔΙΑΔΡΟΜΗ ΠΟΥ ΣΑΣ ΠΡΟΤΕΙΝΟΥΜΕ

Keep following the map on the inside back cover from ❹ to ㉝ and use the **step by step walking guide** and **photo tour** all the way around. **It will bring you back to Ognistra taverna** near where you parked your car or arrived on foot.
To familiarize yourself, look at the map on the inside back cover to see where you are, and where you are going.

A Short Tour Σύντομη ξενάγηση
Alternately, if you don't have much time, take the **short walk** from ❹ to ㉑ as shown on the map inside the back cover. Then simply return to the start via one of the two paths from the Square back to where you began. This is very easy, you will get a good 'highlights' view of the immediate village, and it only takes between 20 - 30 mins.

㉞ **At the end of the suggested circular walk**, we have included an option to take the peripheral road that leads up to **Mount Pantokrator**, but this may need two or three hours there and back (and proper walking gear!) We will tell you more about this walk at the end of the main Old Perithia tour.

THE HOLY CHURCH OF SAINT IAKOVOS, PERSIS ❹

Η ΕΚΚΛΗΣΙΑ ΤΟΥ ΑΓΙΟΥ ΙΑΚΩΒΟΥ ΤΟΥ ΠΕΡΣΗ

With its striking pink belfry and position at the start of the village **The Holy Church of Iakovos, Persis** ❹ is undoubtedly one of the most iconic of the eight churches. Although the church is not open to the public at the moment (restoration is in process) it's filled with beautiful frescoes and original features, some of which have remained relatively intact.

The procession for **The Miracle** commences from here on alternate years, and from **St. Nikolaos, Petra** every other year. The procession then passes all the other churches in the village. The Miracle is so called as the prayers were answered to save the children of the village from a 'mysterious' illness that was taking so many young lives (although it was probably diphtheria).

The inscription on the belfry reads:
This church building was funded by the brothers and parishioners of this Holy House of God. The parishioners are: Nikolaos Kasaris Onoufrios Tserkanos Konstantinos Kasaris Ioannis Tsirgotis. It was finished in August 1833

The Holy Church of St. Iakovos, Persis ❹ Η εκκλησία του Αγίου Ιακώβου του Πέρση

The Miracle

Το θαύμα

The Procession for The Miracle Το θαύμα

On **the last Sunday in July**, the village comes alive with a procession to commemorate the miracle of The Virgin Mary. In 1863, many children in the village suddenly and inexplicably died of a mysterious disease (probably now believed to have been diphtheria). The entire village prayed to God for a miracle and turned to The Virgin Mary for help.
The villagers formed a procession and walked around the village carrying her icon whilst praying with 'an intense faith'.

The following day their prayers were answered and a miracle took place. The disease receded and within a few days it had left the village. From then on and to this day, every year a special procession takes place in honour of The Virgin Mary. Before 1913 it traditionally took place at the end of May.
From 1914 until the liberation from the German occupation, it took place at the end of June. Since the liberation, the commemoration takes place each year on the last Sunday of July.

The following day their prayers were answered and a miracle took place.

The procession commences from **The Holy Church of St. Nikolaos, Petra** one year, and from **The Holy Church of St. Iakovos, Persis** the next, alternating from one year another. The procession then goes through the village and passes every one of its churches for a special invocation to summon The Virgin Mary's continued protection over the village.

Photograph: Courtesy of Mihalis Kokkalis

MAP AND PATH TO KRINIAS & THE OLD SPRING ❺

ΧΑΡΤΗΣ ΚΑΙ ΜΟΝΟΠΑΤΙ ΠΡΟΣ ΚΡΙΝΙΑ & ΤΗΝ ΠΑΛΙΑ ΠΗΓΗ

Map and path to Krinias - Χάρτης και μονοπάτι προς Κρινία

To your right, you'll see the path that leads down to the village of Krinias. Krinias is approx. 4km (1 hour) walk from here. This is one of the eight original settlements that lie beneath Old Perithia. Families from these settlements built homes higher up to grow crops and tend their livestock in the summer, returning to their villages below in the winter.

To see the **Old Spring ❺ follow this path for approximately 1 or 2**

minutes and **take the right fork.** At the end, you'll find the spring and pump used for drawing up the pure and refreshing mountain water. Have a go at the pump (gently) and taste it!

On the page opposite, you can read about the discovery of the village spring back in the early 14th century.

The left fork in the path continues along the old track leading down to Krinias and used to be known as Kakoskala (the difficult passage). Many years ago, before the main road was built, this used to be the only way to reach Old Perithia.

In more recent years, before the village was virtually abandoned, the villagers would travel once or twice a week along this path, by mule or on foot, to buy their groceries and other necessities that were not readily available. This often meant an exhausting two hour round trip. After **Krinias** the road continues down to the coast.

From here retrace your steps back towards the path alongside Ognistra taverna.

The Story of the Old Perithia Spring

Η ιστορία της πηγής της Παλιάς Περίθειας

In 1347, when the village of Old Perithia was established, fresh water was in short supply. The villagers had to collect rainwater or suffer a long trek on foot to the settlements below.

During one hot summer, a local goatherd noticed that one male goat would often 'go missing' and, some while later, re-appear back amongst the herd.

His curiosity aroused, he gathered the villagers, the priest and the mayor, and they followed the herd to see where it was going. Sure enough, the male goat wandered off and disappeared into some thick mountain undergrowth, only to emerge, 10 minutes later… with droplets of crystal clear water falling from his beard.

To the astonishment and delight of the entire village, the goat had discovered a natural spring of clear mountain water.

Now, seven centuries later, from an area of outstanding natural beauty, the 'Old Perithia Spring' still provides pure mountain spring water to the goats, the village, and to all who are fortunate enough to discover it.

The Old Perithia Spring ❺ Η πηγή της Παλιάς Περίθειας

OGNISTRA TAVERNA, 1872 ❻

ΟΓΝΙΣΤΡΑ ΤΑΒΕΡΝΑ

Ognistra taverna ❻ Ταβέρνα 'Ογνίστρα'.

From **Ognistra taverna** at the top of the village, and the **Church of St. Paraskevi** (to the side), you can **follow the suggested full circular tour**, or you can do the '**quick tour**', highlighted on the **map in the inside back cover.**

Ognistra taverna (owned by Nikos Chirdaris) has been beautifully restored using local traditional limestone. This is a good example of how stone buildings would have looked centuries ago.

The name Ognistra translates as 'fireplace' (ognistra, gonistra) and 'corner in the house' (gonia) where Nikos' grandmother used to make fire and cook traditional Corfiot dishes. He spent a lot of his childhood in the village (and has many tales about its history). His parents were educated at **The Old School** (originally **Skordilis Mansion**), which you will see in a short while.

Nikos continues to use the same recipes for his 'home-cooked' food that have passed through the generations, using local

An original style water jug used to collect water from the spring nearby ❻ Αυθεντική κανάτα νερού

Above the entrance to Ognistra taverna, 1872 ❻. One of the restored shuttered windows.
Ταβέρνα 'Ογνίστρα'.

produce and baking his own bread in the 'gonistra'. **Ognistra** is one of only 25 restaurants in the Ionian region to have won the triple merit 'Best Quality' award.
Ognistra taverna
☎ (+30) 26630 98050.

From here, we will guide you around the village, along winding **cobbled stone streets** (saltsada), **farm tracks** or **little alleyways**, over 60 percent of which are from the original settlement.

We will highlight the most historic buildings and points of interest set amongst the many, now deserted, homes.

Keep following the tour all the way around and it will bring you back to The Holy Church of St. Iakovos, Persis ❹ at the end.

Alternatively, if you don't have much time, take the short walk from here ❻ to point ㉑ as shown on the map on the inside back cover.

Then simply return to the start via one of the paths that will lead you back past Ognistra taverna where your walk began. This is very easy and you'll get a good 'highlights' view of the village.

As you walk around, you will notice how a few of the once derelict houses are now under restoration, primarily at the top of the village where the walk starts by The Holy Church of St. Iakovos, Persis.

The Municipality's 'preservation order' requires that properties must be restored within strict guidelines throughout, and with a consistency of architectural standards.

The majority of houses were built by hand with limestone from the local quarries beneath Mount Pantokrator. Some have painted façades, others exposed stonework, a tradition that continues with restorations to this day.

Tavernas
Ταβέρνες

If you wish to grab something to eat or drink before or after your walk, then there's a choice of tavernas in the village that are open every day throughout the summer. In the winter, the tavernas are open almost every weekend. One of the most popular occasions for the Corfiots is Sunday lunch, outside on a shaded terrace or, in the winter, inside a cosy taverna next to a warm fire.

Please Note:
Παρακαλώ σημειώστε

At this stage of the walk, **follow our suggested route** and not the sign to the **Village Square**, or you will miss an important section of the tour. **We'll be passing through The Square along the suggested route later, so you won't miss anything!**

THE HOLY CHURCH OF SAINT PARASKEVI ❼

Η ΕΚΚΛΗΣΙΑ ΤΗΣ ΑΓΙΑΣ ΠΑΡΑΣΚΕΥΗΣ

The Holy Church of St. Paraskevi ❼ is one of the three family owned churches in the village. Over the years many of the churches have been restored, perhaps most recently between the 18th and 19th centuries. In this particular church, the frescoes are still intact.

To the right-hand side, you can see the bare remains of a small house, and, if you look carefully, you can still make out an old oven in the corner. Practically all of the houses in Old Perithia had their own wood ovens.

The Holy Church of St. Paraskevi ❼ Η εκκλησία της Αγίας Παρασκευής

On the main track, as you pass Ognistra taverna, the road soon forks to the left. There is also a path through the gap between the two buildings in front of you that will lead you to **Skordilis Mansion** 'The Old School'.

Now return to the main track to continue the tour.

Keep this in mind, as you will pass through this gap in a short while.

First, there are a few things to see before you take that path, so let's continue the tour.

Take some time to look around these two houses and the far courtyard ❽ and then take a short pause to look at the side wall of these two houses, just before the gap along the side of the Education Centre that leads to Skordilis Mansion. **The history of the houses and their courtyard is examined on the opposite page.**

The path that leads to Skordilis Mansion Το μονοπάτι που οδηγεί στο αρχοντικό Σκορδίλη

TWO FAMILY HOMES AND COURTYARD 8

ΔΥΟ ΟΙΚΟΓΕΝΕΙΑΚΕΣ ΚΑΤΟΙΚΙΕΣ ΚΑΙ ΠΡΟΑΥΛΙΟ

The tree in the picture below grows on one of two pillars in the far corners that would have supported the roof of a veranda. You can still make out the **Courtyard** 8 in front of the farthest house, which, in the past, used to be a **kafeneion.** At night it was often filled with the sound of live music and the villagers used to dance in this courtyard!

Just by the path (that you will take in a moment) look at the sidewall here and you will see that a first floor extension was built onto the previous roof (c. 17th century). The old roofline can be clearly seen along with an old window that was filled in at the time of the extension. Note, the small 'square' holes on the exterior walls around the village, these were used for wooden scaffolding, as these stone houses were all built by hand. Although these two houses are derelict, many features remain intact.

You will see some more of the original features at the rear of these houses when you pass to side of the Education Centre as we return here shortly.

But first, walk a short way along the main track to look at the front of the 'Merchant's House' and the small taverna just beyond on the same path.

Note the old roofline in the centre of the stone side wall 8 Προσέξτε την άκρη της παλιάς στέγης στο κέντρο του πέτρινου τοίχου

Two family homes and courtyard 8 Δύο οικογενειακές κατοικίες και προαύλιο

Music and Dancing Μουσική και χορός

"Cheered with wine the countrymen form into sets, and dance the Romaica in rings, averaging from twenty to thirty in number, each man holding his neighbour's handkerchief; and, beginning with a gradual cadence, they finally whirl around at a rapid pace, which presently evinces a necessity for fresh libations. It is on such occasions that the women display their beautiful native costumes; and, every village having adopted one of its own, the variety gives off a most pleasing effect."

Extract from 'The History of the island of Corfu' by H. Jervis-White Jervis published in 1852.

In years gone by, there was music and dancing in the courtyard 8 Στα παλιά χρόνια το προαύλιο γέμιζε από μουσική και χορό

THREE TRADITIONAL VILLAGE HOUSES: 'THE MERCHANT'S HOUSE' ❾

ΤΡΙΑ ΠΑΡΑΔΟΣΙΑΚΑ ΣΠΙΤΙΑ: 'ΤΟ ΕΜΠΟΡΙΚΟΝ'

These **three traditional houses** ❾ sit side by side with their stone steps leading from the front of the houses down to the road. Their restoration began in 2010.

These village **houses** originally used all of the top floors as accommodation. Below, in the first house, was a traditional '**weavers**' making woollen clothes and rugs out of the wool from local sheep. Next door, in the middle house, was a '**grocery**' selling sugar, coffee, honey and dried fish. The third house in the row was a small but bustling '**kafeneion**' (coffee house). They are all being beautifully restored to their former glory as, **'The Merchant's House' Boutique Bed & Breakfast** Old Perithia ❾ To Εμπορικόν.

Just beyond 'The Merchant's House' is a small pretty taverna called **Gabriel's Steps**.

Now walk a short way back up the track and proceed through the gap by the Education Centre ❿.

Please Note:
(Παρακαλώ σημειώστε)
At this stage of the walk, follow our suggested route below and not the sign and path to the Village Square, or you miss an important section of the tour. We'll pass through The Square along the suggested route later, so you won't miss anything!

Gabriel's Steps taverna
Ταβέρνα «Η σκάλα του Γαβρίλη»

Three traditional village houses, 'The Merchant's House' ⑨ Τρία παραδοσιακά σπίτια, «Το Εμπορικόν»

The Merchant's House

The Merchant's House are Boutique Bedroom Suites including traditional Corfiot breakfast at Ognistra taverna. Traditional hospitality, with a contemporary standard of comfort.

The Merchant's House, Old Perithia, 49081 Corfu
www.MerchantsHouseCorfu.com ☎ (+30) 6988 712 885 or in person at Ognistra Taverna, Old Perithia, Corfu.
stay@merchantshousecorfu.com

Old Weaving Tools Παλιά εργαλεία ύφανσης

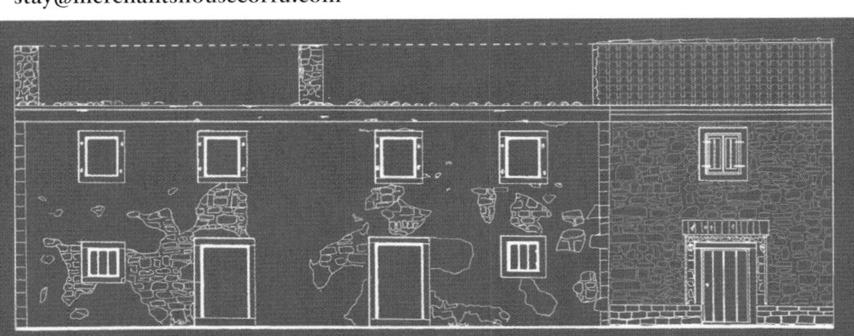

The 'Merchant's House' 9 Το Εμπορικόν

THE EDUCATION CENTRE 

ΤΟ ΚΕΝΤΡΟ ΕΚΠΑΙΔΕΥΣΗΣ

The restored **Education Centre** ⑩ is owned by the Municipality. It plays host to educational visits and environmental studies so, in some way, bringing a '**new school**' back to the village, notably with its proximity to **The Old School** (Skordilis Mansions) to the right and just ahead of you.

The Education Centre ⑩ Το Κέντρο Εκπαίδευσης

As you look at the back of the two old houses, notice the original stonework on either side showing their height before they were extended. Also, clearly visible beneath the frame of the stone window, at the far end, a shelf for potted plants or flowers.

The back of the two family homes and a 'window box' for flowers. Το πίσω μέρος δύο οικογενειακών κατοικιών και ζαρντινιέρα παραθύρου.

With the recent rebuilding, and renovation of many properties at the top of the village, it is probable that further restorations will follow.

There have been suggestions that the overhead telephone wires should be placed underground, that the cobbled stone streets should be repaired. Also, that **The Skordilis Mansion** should be restored to its former glory. But, to this day, the village of Old Perithia is still waiting for these plans to materialise.

However, a firm initiative is under way from The Architectural Department in Corfu for the restoration of **The Holy Church of Iakovos, Persis**. There is also the prospect of a museum showing the history of the village. All of this will further enable both inhabitants and visitors to wander through the village and experience life as it was many centuries ago - a happy and thriving community.

THE 'LODGE' ⓫

Η 'ΕΡΓΑΤΙΚΗ ΚΑΤΟΙΚΙΑ'

Although they may not have been connected, it is possible that this small cottage may have been a 'Lodge' ⓫ or labourer's house, as it is positioned at the side of the entrance to Skordilis residence (latterly the Old School) and extends into the grounds. The noble families of the village often owned and provided homes for the labourers, farmers and their families.

Glance back to your left when you've passed through the arch, and if you look from the arch to the Mansion, you will notice the line of a wall running through the gardens between the house and Mansion. This once separated the gardens between the two properties. About half way along, there was probably an entrance through the wall to the side garden of Skordilis Mansion. Again, you can see a medley of small cottages nearby (probably more estate buildings).

The 'Lodge' ⓫ to the left of The Skordilis Mansion house, gardens and courtyard, latterly 'The Old School'. Η 'εργατική κατοικία'- αργότερα 'Το παλιό σχολείο'

> *"Happy is the man whose labours bring good to his fellows."*
> Greek inscription

THE GRAND ENTRANCE ⓬ ARCH TO SKORDILIS MANSION (THE OLD SCHOOL)

Η ΜΕΓΑΛΗ ΑΨΙΔΑ ΣΤΗΝ ΕΙΣΟΔΟ ΤΟΥ ΑΡΧΟΝΤΙΚΟΥ ΣΚΟΡΔΙΛΗ (ΤΟ ΠΑΛΙΟ ΣΧΟΛΕΙΟ)

Skordilis family crest 'Escutcheon' ⓬ in the centre of the arch
Το οικόσημο της οικογένειας Σκορδίλη

THE VIGLA ⓭ AND OLIVE PRESS ⓮

Η ΒΙΓΛΑ ΚΑΙ ΤΟ ΕΛΑΙΟΠΙΕΣΤΗΡΙΟ

The **Vigla** ⓭ was originally thought to have been approximately 4m high. This rectangular tower was often used as an observation point from which to 'look out' for Pirates. As you will see when you stand there, it is a good viewing position for looking across the mountains, down to the sea.

The Skordilis Mansion was subsequently built many years after the The Vigla was erected. The pictures below show how it may have looked centuries ago.

Curiously, you will see that the bedroom windows to the right-hand side of the mansion are somewhat higher than '**The Vigla**' and their view far exceeds that of the original 'look out' tower. But thankfully, these days they don't have any more pirate attacks!

Just by the Vigla is an **Old Olive Press** ⓮ practically buried in the grass.

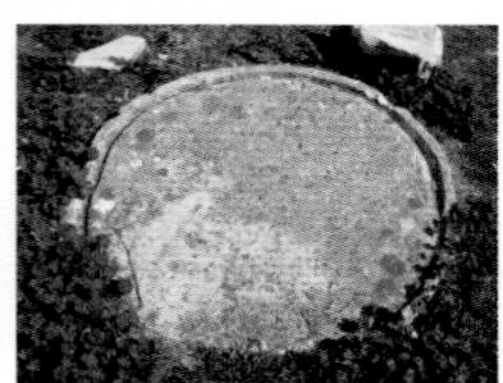

The Vigla ⓭ (look-out tower) now and as it would have looked, and remains of an old olive press in the grounds of Skordilis Mansion ⓮ Η βίγλα και τα απομεινάρια παλιού ελαιοπιεστηρίου στο αρχοντικό Σκορδίλη

SKORDILIS MANSION 'THE OLD SCHOOL' ⑮

ΤΟ ΑΡΧΟΝΤΙΚΟ ΣΚΟΡΔΙΛΗ "ΤΟ ΠΑΛΙΟ ΣΧΟΛΕΙΟ"

Skordilis Mansion, also known as 'The Old School', ⑮ was built in 1699 and is surrounded by a (once, walled) garden. It belonged to the wealthy Skordilis family. The entrance (portoni) consisted of a gate with a marble arch and the family coat of arms (escutcheon).

Both the arch and coat of arms have suffered from the weather over the years, but they are still standing.

The building was latterly owned by the Papadatos family until **1817**, when it was sold (for just 1600 drachma's) to the Church community of Old Perithia for use as a 'summer' school when the families lived and worked in the village.

The Old School remained until **1940.** The ground floor was converted into two offices and a classroom. The first floor had a single classroom and the rooms at the back became the headmaster's office. The headmaster also used the old mansion as a home.

On the outside there were originally ornate marble columns on the arch and outer staircase leading to the upper floor. The balcony had a traditional Corfiot stone seat. But this, along with other marble facings was stolen when the building was abandoned.

Skordilis Mansion 'The Old School' ⑮ Το αρχοντικό Σκορδίλη 'Το παλιό σχολείο'

The Skordilis Mansion and grounds are among the most substantial in the village, along with Chirdaris, Sarakinos and Salvanos Mansions.

The **Church of St. Panteleimonas ⑯** is situated just behind **Skordilis Mansion**, a short walk away.

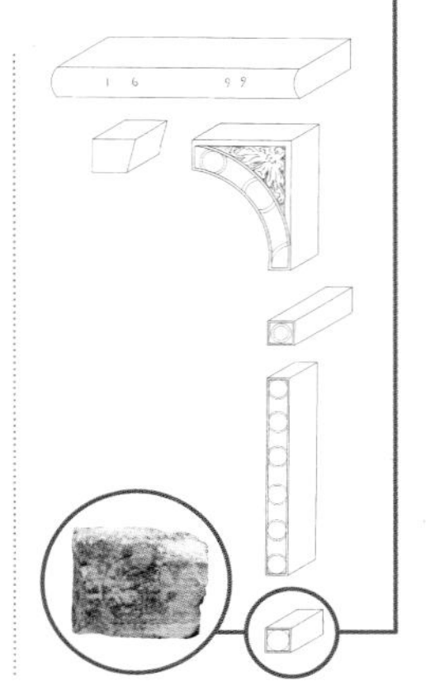

The Skordilis Family

Η οικογένεια Σκορδίλη

The first Skordilis family were of Byzantine aristocracy, sent out from Constantinople to Crete as administrators around 1180. When Crete fell to the Turks, this famous Cretan family was dispersed.

One of them, the Military Doctor Pieros Skordilis, had relations with a powerful Corfiot noble house, having married its heiress Paolini Palatsouol. Pieros sought from the ruling Venetians, estates and property comparable to what he had left behind in Crete, offering in exchange a few zecchini (Venetian gold coins) probably just enough to cover the costs of drawing up the contracts. In 1692, he was accepted, by exception, into the noble families of Corfu.

The couple owned much property, scattered among the many villages, including Skordilis Mansion, built in Old Perithia in 1699. Their granddaughter, Setsilia Palatasouol-Skordilis, married the Viscount Francesco Balbi, who offered to Venice the services of his armour-plated ship which he captained himself on patrol in the Ionian sea. It was Francesco who inherited the whole fortune of the family.

Pieros had two sons, Janetos and Georgis. The latter, a doctor like his father, married the wealthy Diamantina Karmary from Corfu. Many Skordilis families were registered in Corfu under the name Skordou.

The estate passed though the generations and, after the Corfu Land Act of 1912, much land was surrendered to the local peasants who worked it.

The Skordilis family emblem, which they brought from Crete, was the lion brandishing a sword, but it was not their coat of arms, which featured a garlic bulb (skordo). The Palatsouol coat of arms bore a palace and a sun (palazzo and sole) and that of the Balbi family a faggot of sticks tied together, symbolising their unity.

Many of their family papers and correspondence still exist, including the notification from the People's Republic of Venice to the nobleman Veneto Francesco Balbi informing him of the removal of his rank and addressing him as a citizen 'cittadino' now that the aristocracy 'has finally expired' as described at that time.

The Cretan Lion

The family are distinguished for cherishing their history, their roots, their traditions, documents and official records, not for their love of money.

Extracts from Noble Houses of Corfu by Despina Paisidou.
Additional information kindly provided by Loukas Skordilis and his family in Corfu.

Photograph: The Cretan Lion, courtesy of Wilma and Dimitri Zervos

THE HOLY CHURCH OF SAINT PANTELEIMONAS ⑯ AND FRESCOES

Η ΕΚΚΛΗΣΙΑ ΤΟΥ ΑΓΙΟΥ ΠΑΝΤΕΛΕΗΜΟΝΑ ΚΑΙ ΤΟΙΧΟΓΡΑΦΙΕΣ

Walk to the left side of Skordilis Mansion and then slightly up to the right to a little church. **This is the Church of St. Panteleimonas ⑯.**

Unusually, you will approach the church from the back, whereas you would think that the entrance should face Skordilis Mansion. You may also have noticed this as you walked towards 'the back' of St. Paraskevi next to the first taverna.

What is fascinating, particularly from an aerial point of view, is that all of the churches are built on an east-west line with the entrances generally facing east and altars facing west. It explains why you often seem to arrive facing the back of some churches in the village, and have to walk around the church to find the entrance.

You will notice this in particular at **St. Paraskevi, St. Panteleimonas** and **Zoodochos Pigi.** There are also exceptions such as **St. Nikolaos, Petra** with its door at the side.

The churches are deliberately built on an **east-west line** with the entrance of the church on the west side and the altar on the east side. The reason for this is the alignment with the sun, rising in the east and setting in the west.

This construction is of religious significance. The altar is in the east where the sun rises, as God is the rising sun and therefore rises with the sun from the east. In the church burial grounds (and cemeteries) the body is laid the other way around, i.e. the head lays at the west in order to witness the resurrection in the east where the sun rises.

The Church of St. Panteleimonas ⑯ still has some remnants of **frescoes** painted on the walls.

What is fascinating, particularly from an aerial point of view, is that all of the churches are built on an east-west line with the entrances generally facing east and altars facing west.

The Holy Church of St. Panteleimonas ⓰ frescoes inside the church and evidence of the stolen icons. Η εκκλησία του Αγίου Παντελεήμονα

Unfortunately, as you will see, the icons have been taken along with the marble and some of the ancient stones from the floor. One of the saints painted in the left-hand corner has borne witness to those who have stolen from the church. Let's hope that he is there to testify against the thieves when they wish to gain entry to heaven.

The Church of Saint Panteleimonas still has some remnants of the frescoes painted on the walls.

Please Note:
Παρακαλώ σημειώστε
Having visited the church, walk back towards Skordilis Mansion, and then turn right, down to the Old Grocery Shop ⓱ that's in front of you.

THE OLD GROCERY SHOP AND WELL ⑰

ΤΟ ΠΑΛΙΟ ΠΑΝΤΟΠΩΛΕΙΟ ΚΑΙ ΠΗΓΑΔΙ

As well as **'kafeneia'** (coffee shops), there were **'pantopolia'** (grocery shops) which both stocked various local provisions. Locals practically 'lived off the land' as there was such a supply of natural produce surrounding them, but for items that nature didn't provide they would go to a grocery shop or the villages below.

On the ground floor inside this old grocery shop ⑰ you can still see where the groceries and bread were once displayed. There were also two ovens for baking bread. Glancing into the farthest room downstairs you can still see one of the ovens, the second one is now barely visible. Other internal features can still be seen but are suffering with each passing season. As with all the buildings in the village, **please take great care if entering any of the houses.**

The old grocery shop and well ⑰ Το Παλιό Παντοπωλείο και Πηγάδι

The distinct turquoise shutters on the top floor of the old grocery and well, to the side ⑰ Τα χαρακτηριστικά τιρκουάζ παντζούρια στον πάνω όροφο του Παλιού Παντοπωλείου και η Πηγή, στο πλάι

The grocery shop on the ground floor ⓱ Το Παλιό Παντοπωλείο - Παλιός ξύλινος φούρνος

Bakers and Coffee House Keepers
Αρτοποιοί και ιδιοκτήτες καφενείων

The Bakers of Corfu in 1837 petitioned for longer opening hours for their shops and for being allowed to prepare more (white) bread for the affluent classes, the 'classe piu agiata della citta.' The coffee-house keepers claimed that their customers, the 'lowest class of citizens' and the 'working class', would prefer to spend time in their shops than go to Church and petitioned for being allowed to open during the early hours of Sundays and religious holidays, during Mass.

Extract from: Class formation in the Ionian Islands during the period of British rule, 1814-1864 © Dr Sakis Gekas

Many **ovens** on the ground or upper floors of the houses had chimneys. Interestingly though, there were also many indoor ovens with no chimney at all.

Instead a small 'outlet' gently and slowly expelled the smoke. Remarkably this ingenious system didn't fill the room with smoke. This feature is illustrated in the picture (right) where you can see a restored traditional wood oven and the ventilation hole to the left just above.

An old wood oven Παλιός ξύλινος φούρνος

The villagers often made their own bread, so almost every house in Old Perithia had its own wood oven.

Note the 'roof line' that appears across the far side of the building just beneath the window (illustrated above) and the lovely view from the far side, past the wall and well (below).

As the centuries passed, the villagers that wanted bigger homes simply built up onto the roofline. Rather like rings in the horizontal section of an old tree, these illustrate the timelines. The first roofline being approximately 14th or 15th

century, the second, 17th century. Some even had a third in the 19th century.

In the distance, you will see a **red gate** at the entrance to the **olive grove** that you will pass by further along this walk. There are many derelict terraces, which climb like giant size staircases around the village. These once supported flat land for cultivation of crops and now support bees or groves. They act as a reminder and testimony to the formerly thriving farming community of Old Perithia.

In the past, there were herds of sheep, goats, pigs and wild bulls, in Old Perithia. There was also an abundance of wheat and corn terraces, vineyards, fruit trees, wild edible plants and numerous herbs in the surrounding green hills. You can still pick many fruits and 'greens' (Horta) today, but the numbers of sheep, goats and bulls are greatly reduced.

The village was practically a self-sufficient community with 'noblemen' and country folk living side by side.

In centuries past, the grocery and other shops came and went, and the five local kafeneia (coffee houses), were the places to meet for a chat, a drink, maybe coffee, wine or ouzo. You could also buy items such as rice, sugar, coffee and tobacco in the café's, that served the lively local community in this popular mountain hamlet.

A recently planted olive grove seen from the grocery, and old stone house on the way down to the village square ⑱ Ελαιώνας και παλιό πέτρινο σπίτι καθ' οδόν προς την πλατεία του χωριού

From The Old Grocery Shop ⑰ follow the path down past a few deserted houses (there's a a good example of one on your right).

Soon after you will arrive at **The Village Square ⑱**. When you arrive, to your left beneath a large **elm tree**, you'll see **Foros Taverna ⑲**.

You are now standing at a point where three roads meet to encompass **The Village Square ⑱**.

To your right, you will see **The Old Perithia Taverna ⑲** with its pretty terrace and view towards the beautiful **Church of St. Spyridon**.

Apart from the tavernas, the 'square' may appear rather deserted now, except for diners at the surrounding tavernas. Although, in times gone by, dances frequently took place around the elm trees. Nowadays, dancing ordinarily takes place at festival times.

THE VILLAGE SQUARE ⓲

Η ΠΛΑΤΕΙΑ ΤΟΥ ΧΩΡΙΟΥ

It was in this cobbled street that the village's first ever taverna was located, called '**Capricorn**'. The taverna was run by an Ano Perithian and his vivacious Chilean wife. From those who still remember the history of 'Capricorn' at that time, it was apparently quite a unique and lively place. It reopened in 2010 and is right next door to Foros taverna and diagonally opposite The Old Perithia taverna.

The small village square ⓲ is not quite the traditional square you would expect to find in Corfu (surrounded by coffee shops with a central seating area) but it certainly has the feel of a central meeting point for the village with the two elm trees and the three tavernas on either side of the square.

The word '**foros**', derives from the Latin '**forum**' which was an open public square or marketplace in an ancient Roman city (in Italy this would later be called a 'piazza'). The square would be an assembly place for judicial and other public activities or meetings and, of course, much dancing!

FOROS TAVERNA AND TERRACE ⓳

ΤΑΒΕΡΝΑ ΚΑΙ ΑΥΛΗ "Ο ΦΟΡΟΣ"

Foros taverna ⓳ ☎ (+30) 6943 100510. This taverna, shaded by one of the two elm trees, sits in the village square '**Foros Square**' and is run by Tomas and Vasso Siriotis. They serve traditional Corfiot food from a small kitchen up a flight of rickety old stairs.

In the shade of the two big **elm trees** by the village square, you can see an **interesting cluster of angled roofs** on houses next to, and visible from, **The Old Perithia and Foros** taverna terraces (see picture to the right).

Foros taverna and terrace ⓳ Ταβέρνα και Αυλή «Ο Φόρος»

THE OLD PERITHIA TAVERNA ⑳

ΤΑΒΕΡΝΑ "Η ΠΑΛΙΑ ΠΕΡΙΘΕΙΑ"

The Old Perithia Taverna ⑳ and vines on their terrace. Ταβέρνα «Η Παλιά Περίθεια» και κληματαριά στην αυλή.

The Old Perithia taverna ⑳ ☎ (+30) 26630 98055 with its attractive vine-covered terrace has been owned by the same family since 1863. It was originally a **kafeneion** (coffee house) that also served a small selection of food. **The Old Perithia** taverna ⑳ has a warm and friendly atmosphere and a fascinating collection of photos and memorabilia in the restaurant area indoors. It is run by Alkinoos Kassaris, the great grandson of the original owner, and his family.

Open all summer, and winter (at weekends). On the old elm tree by the entrance, there is a '**tap**'

once used for washing your hands and face. From the edge of the outside seating area it has great views of St. Spyridon.

THE SUNDIAL ㉑

ΤΟ ΗΛΙΑΚΟ ΡΟΛΟΙ

Opposite the entrance to The Old Perithia taverna you will see a small cobbled street. **Take a 30 second walk** up this path, and above you on the wall of what was once the 'noble' house of the Boletsis family is a **Sundial ㉑** on the faded wall above. **Compare the time with that on your watch!**

The next house along, is the now indistinguishable **Old Town Hall**, but do still take a peek inside. In the past all the lower floors (katoi) or basements were shops or stores that lined the bustling cobbled streets around the square.

There was no police station nor court in Old Perithia, the nearest police station was based in the village of Loutses.

After The Sundial ㉑ turn back and proceed back past the left side of The Old Perithia taverna and down towards the **Church of St. Spyridon ㉒**. Ahead of you, its pure white silhouette radiates with the reflection of the sun.

The Sundial
Το ηλιακό ρολόι

For centuries, sundials have been used to mark the passage of time while reminding us of the rhythms of our universe. The gnomon is the part of the sundial that casts the shadow. Gnomon (Γνώμων) is an ancient Greek word meaning 'indicator', or 'that which reveals'. Roman writers give evidence of their acquisition of this instrument from the Greeks.

Photograph: Courtesy of Alkistis Prepis

The Sundial ㉑ and an internal staircase in the Old Town Hall next door Το Ηλιακό Ρολόι και εσωτερική σκάλα στο Παλιό Δημαρχείο

To continue the recommended circular tour (after looking around), go back past the left side of The Old Perithia taverna and walk down towards the white church of St Spyridon.

If you are taking the short tour, continue past the **sundial** along the path towards the top of the village.

This path will bring you back past Gabriel's Steps and 'The Merchant's House' on your right, and then back up to Ognistra taverna.

THE HOLY CHURCH OF SAINT SPYRIDON ㉒ ㉓

Η ΕΚΚΛΗΣΙΑ ΤΟΥ ΑΓΙΟΥ ΣΠΥΡΙΔΩΝΑ

The Holy Church of St. Spyridon ㉒ and its unusual green door, seen as you arrive at the side entrance to the church. Η εκκλησία του Αγίου Σπυρίδωνα και η ασυνήθιστη πράσινη πόρτα της, όπως φαίνεται από την πλάγια είσοδο της εκκλησίας.

When you arrive at the **Church of St. Spyridon** ㉒, a family owned church, look at the unusual **green door** at the side and pretty small stained glass window above to the right. Then **pass through the attractive arched belfry** and past the entrance door, avoiding any straying chickens that are sometimes to be seen there!

Continue onwards up the path that curves to the right. You will see a stepped wall (for crops or olive groves) and stone steps leading to the side ahead of you - stay on the pathway.

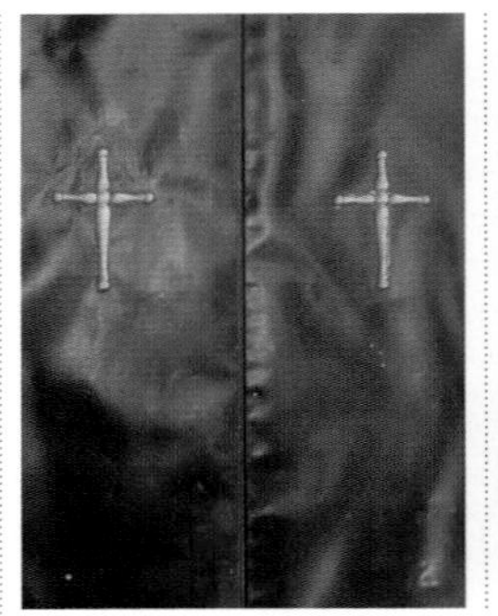

Walking through the belfry of the church of St. Spyridon ㉒
Περνώντας από το καμπαναριό του Αγίου Σπυρίδωνα

Look at the unusual green door at the side and simple small stained glass window above to the right.

Photograph (top of page): Courtesy of Mihalis Kokkalis

As you continue walking up the pathway, look back up at the houses you've passed, you get an excellent snapshot of a cluster of the old houses.

The old photo (above), dating from approximately 30 years ago, illustrates how different and impressive the village once looked, as seen beyond the roof and chimney pots of a simple countryman's house in the foreground.

The grocery with its turquoise shutters can also be seen from the pathway. During its heyday Old Perithia was a thriving community, attracting many visitors from the villages nearby.

You will pass a red gate at the entrance to a recently planted Olive Grove ㉓ **and here the pathway veers to the left.**

Along the way there are one or two houses either side of the path, some restored, some in need of restoration.

Continue on the path ahead and you will approach a single cypress tree that indicates your arrival at the ochre coloured church of Zoodochos Pigi ㉔ visible just to your right, set upon a carpet of lush green grass.

This family-owned church is in good condition and looks so attractive in its contrasting and vibrant green surroundings.

THE HOLY CHURCH OF ZOODOCHOS PIGI ㉔

Η ΕΚΚΛΗΣΙΑ ΤΗΣ ΖΩΟΔΟΧΟΥ ΠΗΓΗΣ

The Holy Church of Zoodochos Pigi ㉔ Η εκκλησία της Ζωοδόχου Πηγής

For a little detour, continue up the path to your right by the side of this church and you'll come across **Salvanos Mansions** ㉕ which deceptively seems like one single renovation as you approach. **But... walk along the front and keep going** because next to the mansion are a number of these houses which were probably used for the labourers and their families.

This is an impressive row of houses with many original features still intact as shown in the series of pictures (opposite page) including; ovens, the original pillars, verandas and an old door with a hole in the bottom left hand corner - the original **catflap!**

The noble houses in the village had marble arches and external stone stairs leading to a first floor veranda with stone columns (botzos). A perfect example can be seen on the veranda of the farthest of Salvanos' houses. All had wooden roofs laid with Byzantine style tiles. Features included marble columns and frames, around the doors and windows.

SALVANOS MANSIONS ㉕

ΤΟ ΑΡΧΟΝΤΙΚΟ ΣΑΛΒΑΝΟΥ

Salvanos Mansions (above) ㉕ **and** (right) **the pathway to the bees and church of St. Nikolaos, Petra.** Το αρχοντικό Σαλβάνου και μονοπάτι προς τα μελίσσια και την εκκλησία του Αγίου Νικολάου της Πέτρας.

Pillar supporting veranda, old indoor oven, external staircase and an old front door (with catflap) Στύλος για τη στήριξη βεράντας, παλιός εσωτερικός φούρνος, εξωτερική σκάλα και παλιά μπροστινή πόρτα (με πόρτα γάτας).

Now return past the church of Zoodochos Pigi, turn right and continue up the pathway (shown above). Depending on the time of year, you may begin to hear the sound of the bees humming in the trees above you as they collect their nectar. Soon, to your left, you will see the impressive and somewhat mystical looking ruins of Chirdaris Mansions ㉖.

CHIRDARIS MANSIONS ㉖

ΤΟ ΑΡΧΟΝΤΙΚΟ ΧΕΙΡΔΑΡΗ

Though it is often difficult to see through the overgrown gardens that now practically engulf it in the summer, the once noble **Chirdaris Mansion** ㉖ is another example of the significant 'noble mansions' in the village.

Mansions like these were a result of the Venetian era, a remnant of an old-fashioned medieval system that stemmed from the Angevin lords, who ruled the island in the late 13th and early 14th century. It is of a substantial size with a traditional arch in the centre and fascinating architectural details both inside and out.

Such 'noble' houses as this may have been principally used as a base to oversee and to supervise the labourers who worked for them and for the storage of crops. Behind Chirdaris Mansion is **Sarakinos Mansion.** Look around and then continue back along the recommended path. **In the late 18th and early 19th century** the three 'classes' were (to use a contemporary definition) the **'gentilissimi'** or **nobili** (nobles) the **cittadini** citizens or **'signors'** (middle class bourgeoisie) and the **contadini** (peasants) or **popolo** (people, farmers or countrymen).

Chirdaris Mansions ㉖ with its classic arch and grand architectural features. Το αρχοντικό Χειρδάρη με κλασική αψίδα και έντονα αρχιτεκτονικά στοιχεία.

A BEAUTIFULLY RESTORED HOME 27

ΕΝΑ ΟΜΟΡΦΟ ΑΝΑΚΑΙΝΙΣΜΕΝΟ ΣΠΙΤΙ

Continue a little further along the path. When you get to the fork in the path, **keep to the right**, and after approximately 50 metres you will see **a beautifully restored home** 27. In 2002, the typical outer staircase and original features were restored to the way they were a long time ago. **Follow the path on the left past this house** and soon after you'll see the sign for **'honey'** on the houses to your left.

A beautifully restored home 27 retaining its original architectural features such as the external staircases. Ένα όμορφο ανακαινισμένο σπίτι με αυθεντικά αρχιτεκτονικά στοιχεία όπως οι εξωτερικές σκάλες.

The Signors of the late 18th to early 19th century
Οι σινιόροι στα τέλη του 18ου και στις αρχές του 19ου αιώνα

"In private life, the Signor imitates the Italian customs, spending his time at the Casino, and seldom frequenting his home except at meal times. Fond of display, although perhaps living in a garret (top floor or attic room), he will sport his white gloves on the Esplanade, and display his person at the Opera. A gambler to the back-bone, he will in one night, spent at the nobles' club, lose his income of a month, and thereby further mortgage his small patrimony.

Although confined by this narrow spirit to the intercourse of some particular clique, yet, even in this narrow sphere, the Corfiot signor prefers to waste his years, so long as he can live in the capital, leaving his olives and vines to the care of the farmer, who usually tills the land, giving a third of the produce as rent*: but distrust of the tenants' honesty usually induces the landlord to visit the country while the crops are being gathered, to see he is not defrauded of his fair portion."

[*This mode of farming has prevailed from the earliest period.]

Extract from 'The History of the island of Corfu' H. Jervis-White Jervis published in 1852.

THE 'WILD HONEY' SIGNS ON THE BUILDING AND THYME-COVERED SIDE ENTRANCE TO THE HIVES ㉘

Η ΕΠΙΓΡΑΦΗ "ΑΓΡΙΟ ΜΕΛΙ" ΣΤΟ ΚΤΙΡΙΟ ΚΑΙ Η ΚΑΛΥΜΜΕΝΗ ΜΕ ΘΥΜΑΡΙ ΕΙΣΟΔΟΣ ΠΡΟΣ ΤΑ ΜΕΛΙΣΣΙΑ

Thyme for Honey
Θυμάρι για μέλι

You cannot fail to hear the bees, or see **the signs** on the house **to your left** where a beekeeper keeps his hives.

If the beekeeper is there, stop for a short while and buy a jar of truly organic honey, infused with the flavour and scent of all that Mother Nature, the mountains and Old Perithia have to offer. The beekeeper **Spiros** may even tell you a few stories about the Old Village. It's a wonderful experience to sit amidst the hum and the homes of the bees, as they pass by, catching seconds of your conversation, and you, of theirs!

The 'wild honey' signs on the building and thyme covered side entrance to the hives ㉘ on the hairpin bend in the path. Η επιγραφή «άγριο μέλι» στο κτίριο και η καλυμμένη με θυμάρι είσοδος προς τα μελίσσια στην στροφή του μονοπατιού.

The Beehives. Behind, the beekeepers house with three roof lines visible to the side from the 15th, 17th and 19th centuries ㉘. Τα μελίσσια. Από πίσω, το σπίτι του μελισσοκόμου με τρεις οροφές, διακριτές από το πλάι 15ος, 17ος και 19οςαιώνας.

THE HOLY CHURCH OF SAINT NIKOLAOS, PETRA ㉙

Η ΕΚΚΛΗΣΙΑ ΤΟΥ ΑΓΙΟΥ ΝΙΚΟΛΑΟΥ ΤΗΣ ΠΕΤΡΑΣ

The Holy Church of St. Nikolaos, Petra ㉙ Η εκκλησία του Αγίου Νικολάου της Πέτρας

The Holy Church of St. Nikolaos, Petra ㉙ (once a female monastery) welcomes you with its long stone stairs leading through a portico (at one time decorated with a square fresco) and up to the red entrance door at the side, and belfry to the left. The renovation of this church started in 2009, first of all with a new roof and there are plans to restore the original features.

The cypress trees either side of the belfry evoke a feeling of a Tuscan village. In the old days, there used to be an entrance with engraved marble and columns. This is the only one of the eight churches that was built, and is owned by the Perithiotes.

The churches of St. Spyridon, Paraskevi and Zoodochos Pigi are all family owned. The remaining four churches are now under the community of Loutses, albeit that they are all located in and around the village of Old Perithia.

Photograph: Courtesy of Mihalis Kokkalis

The Holy Church of St. Nikolaos, Petra 29 Η εκκλησία του Αγίου Νικολάου της Πέτρας

If you fancy a short break, find a comfortable place to sit and take a few moments to read about all the churches in the next few pages. If you want to keep going then skip to page 70, walk back down the stairs from **St. Nikolaos, Petra** and continue with the tour.

THE EIGHT CHURCHES AT THE FOOT OF THE ALMIGHTY

ΟΙ ΟΚΤΩ ΕΚΚΛΗΣΙΕΣ ΣΤΟΥΣ ΠΡΟΠΟΔΕΣ ΤΟΥ ΠΑΝΤΟΚΡΑΤΟΡΑ

The eight churches served an estimated community of around 1100 people, living in 130 houses. Apart from this being an indication of a deep religious faith, it is also an indicator of the historic significance of this small community.

As mentioned in the introduction, the churches are all built on an east-west line, with the entrances

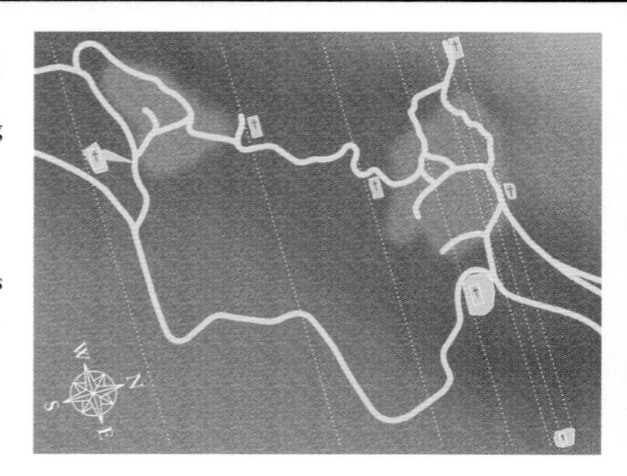

Old Perithia is therefore a village 'Surrounded by The Divine.'

'Περικυκλωμένη από τον Παντοκράτορα.'

generally facing east and the altars facing west. This explains why you often seem to arrive at the back of some churches in the village, and have to walk around the church to find the entrance.

You will notice this in particular at **St. Paraskevi, St. Panteleimonas** and **Zoodochos Pigi**. There are also exceptions such as **St. Nikolaos, Petra** with its door at the side.

The churches are deliberately built on an **east west line** with the entrance of the church on the west side and the altar on the east side.

The reason for this is the alignment with the sun, rising in the east and setting in the west.

The altar is in the east where the sun rises. God is the rising sun, and therefore rises with the sun from the east.

In the church burial grounds (and cemeteries) the body is laid the other way around, i.e. with the head at the west, in order to witness the resurrection (rising of the sun) in the east. Interestingly these churches were built in a near circular layout around the village. **Old Perithia** (peri theia) is so named because the village is, as it were, '**surrounded by the divine**' and set beneath the monastery of Mount Pantokrator, '**at the foot of God**'.

The churches of Old Perithia are particularly impressive, not only for their architecture but also by their number.

The monastery at the top of **Mount Pantokrator** was built in 1347, around the same year that **Old Perithia** was first recorded. When the original monastery, dedicated to Christ Pantokrator **'The Almighty'**, was built the name was applied to the entire mountain. Over the centuries, the original structures have been replaced a number of times but were destroyed sometime around 1537. The current church on the site dates from around 1689, and the current façade was built during the 19th century.

A simple church window Απλό παράθυρο εκκλησίας

The eight churches and bell towers that surround **Old Perithia** are generally of post-Byzantine style, with some renovation features from around 1792 and 1833 (i.e. the churches of **St. Nikolaos, Petra** and of **St. Iakovos, Persis** respectively).

If you look inside some of the chapels, you may be able to see some remarkable frescoes and icons of the saints. The entrances to the churches were often decorated with marble. Unfortunately, many of the antiquities and religious icons were stolen or destroyed as the village was often raided after its desertion.

Symbol on an old church gate - Σύμβολο που κοσμεί την είσοδο παλιάς εκκλησίας

Many of the churches within the village have been painted over the past 50 years and now stand attractively amongst the many stone houses and local landscape.

The churches are basilicas (oblong buildings) of Byzantine origin and two are with vaulted roofs. The belfries are especially interesting, taking the form of either a high-perforated wall or a tower. Over the years, most have been redecorated, rebuilt or restored in their time-honoured style, perhaps most recently between the 18th and 19th centuries.

The bells, the bells
Οι καμπάνες, οι καμπάνες

To a stranger in Corfu, there is perhaps no nuisance more intolerable than the constant ringing of church bells. It is a saying on the islands, that there are as many churches as houses; and the exaggeration is not very great. But the sound that greets the ear, is not the solemn peal from some venerated cathedral, or homely chime of the village church. It is a heathenish tom-tom, generally caused by a small boy, who, grasping the tongues of two small bells, rattles away at them until absolute exhaustion compels him to desist. These engines of auricular torture rattle on Sundays, and on festival days. If it be a proprietary chapel, the din is renewed on the occasion of every birth, death, and marriage in the family. The consequence is, that, day or night there is incessantly some bell twinkling violently in the immediate neighbourhood.

Extract from 'The History of the island of Corfu' by H. Jervis-White Jervis published in 1852.

St. Nikolaos, Petra Ο Άγιος Νικόλαος της Πέτρας

Walk back down the steps of the church of **St. Nikolaos, Petra** and **turn right at the bottom** to continue up the path.

A few moments later, you'll see a track immediately to your right. This leads to Mount Pantokrator.

Do not take the right turning (unless you're planning to go up the mountain). Stay on the peripheral track ㉚ back towards Old Perithia.

Before you continue, take a moment to glance back at the **Belfry of St. Nikolaos** ㉙, and the Cypress trees that surround it, pointing towards the sky and set against the background of the mountains.

Then, continue along the path with the village to your left and towards the pink church of Iakovos, Persis in the distance.

As you walk along, stop occasionally to enjoy the many beautiful views of the village, the mountains, the sea beyond and, in closer proximity, the wildlife, flora and fauna.

The views over the next few hundred metres are amongst the best of the tour, and give you a complete perspective of the village and its location.

Looking back from the path at the belfry of St. Nikolaos, Petra ㉙ Το καμπαναριό του Αγίου Νικολάου της Πέτρας όπως φαίνεται από το μονοπάτι, κοιτώντας προς τα πίσω

VIEWS OF OLD PERITHIA ㉚

ΟΨΕΙΣ ΤΗΣ ΠΑΛΙΑΣ ΠΕΡΙΘΕΙΑΣ

Views of Old Perithia ㉚ with the sea in the distance (top) and (below) to the far right, the church belfry of St. Iakovos, Persis Όψεις της Παλιάς Περίθειας με τη θάλασσα στο βάθος και (στη δεύτερη φωτογραφία) στην άκρη δεξιά, η εκκλησία του Αγίου Ιακώβου του Πέρση.

As you continue **along the track and** as you walk back towards the pink **Church of Iakovos, Persis,** there are a few old houses to look at which are scattered to the left and right.

Most impressive of all are the spectacular views **as you wind your way back to the starting point of the walk.**

Take your time
Πάρτε το χρόνο σας

Take your time to look at the trees, plants, flowers, wild herbs, birds, insects and butterflies around you. There are often birds of prey to be seen, hovering in the clear blue sky, and then suddenly swooping down to catch their prey. Swallows and cuckoos are known to build their nests in some of the abandoned houses. In the summer their song can often be heard at night. There's more detail about the wildlife, flora and fauna at the end of the tour section, later in the guide.

Soon, you'll come to a natural curve in the track, with an old stone house to your right on the bend, tiles missing from its roof and ivy spreading unchecked over the walls.

Moments later you will see the rooftop of a house set into the rock ㉛. From here you can see The Church of St. Iakovos, Persis ahead of you in the distance.

House with ivy and the tiled roof of the small house built into the rock ㉛ Σπίτι σκεπασμένο με κισσό και η κεραμιδένια στέγη ενός μικρού σπιτιού χτισμένο στα βράχια

VIEWS ACROSS THE OLD VILLAGE

Η ΘΕΑ ΑΠΟ ΤΟ ΠΑΛΙΟ ΧΩΡΙΟ

Photograph: Courtesy of Mihalis Kokkalis

View across the village. Past and present. Η θέα από το χωριό. Παρελθόν και παρόν.

You are now at a perfect viewing point for seeing the whole village, and the sea in the distance beyond. Do take the opportunity to take an 'aerial' photo from here. The old black and white photo (above) shows how the village looked some years ago and helps you imagine how impressive Old Perithia was many centuries before.

Continue for a few moments towards the next curve in the path and just before you come onto the approach to Iakovos, Persis, you will see what looks like a large single house down to your left. It rises from a lower floor set in the rock, to a top floor which is level with the path ㉜.

THE 'HOUSE WITHIN A HOUSE' ㉜

ΤΟ «ΣΠΙΤΙ ΜΕΣΑ ΣΤΟ ΣΠΙΤΙ»

Many houses were once constructed with one side built into the rock (like the house with the tiled roof a few minutes ago).

The house, that you now see stepped into the rocks ahead, appears to form one large residence which rises from beneath the path to an upper (ground) floor that is level with the path.

Countrymen and their homes, in the late 18th century
Χωρικοί και τα σπίτια τους, στα τέλη του 18ου αιώνα

Cottages, whilst they present a fair exterior, are particularly filthy within; having usually the bare ground for flooring, with a bed and large box for furniture. One circumstance, however, attracts the attention of strangers, and that is the size and the beauty of their beds. This arises from them not being seizable for debt: much money and care is therefore, usually spent upon the adornment of the bed: and the marriage wreath and patron saint are placed over it.

Beyond the bed, however, all attempt at cleanliness or ornament stops; but if their dwellings are dirty, their persons are still dirtier. The countrymen cloth wove at home, from coarse cotton or brown goat hair, by the industrious housewife, furnishes him with ample clothing. The custom of wearing long hair, which is common to both sexes, and prevails universally, affords them not only employment, but amusement; and the stranger who wonders through the country, his own head delightfully swimming with poetical ideas of mountain scenery and azure skies, is somewhat unpleasantly surprised at beholding a living couple under the shade of an olive grove, the man with his head reposing on his fair partner's lap, whilst she is leisurely ridding his bushy locks of their numerous inhabitants.

Extract from 'The History of the island of Corfu' by H. Jervis-White Jervis published in 1852.

The 'house within a house' ㉜ used for livestock and/or chickens - Το «σπίτι μέσα στο σπίτι»

Look at the wall facing the path as you pass by and you can see the outline of what looks like a 'house within a house' ㉜.

This outline indicates where centuries earlier, jutting onto the path of the main house, there was a small 'residence' for the chickens and livestock.

On the opposite side of the path is a small single storey cottage. It wasn't until the mid to late 19th century that many houses were extended upwards, as the income from agriculture and commerce, along with ownership of land, enabled villagers to build bigger homes.

You are now close to the end of the tour

Σύντομα θα ολοκληρώσετε την περιήγησή σας.

Perhaps as you get to the end of the path you may come across the oldest residents of the village, Gerasimos and Stamatella who have been in the village their entire lives. They live in an old house at the end of a small track and produce and sell their own delicious honey and feta ㉝.

You may have seen them earlier, on your way into the village herding the goats across the road not far from the natural entrance to Old Perithia, or on the slopes of Mount Pantokrator where their herds are often grazing.

Ahead, you can clearly see the pink belfry of Iakovos, Persis ❹ and as you continue walking you will pass by the side of this church and arrive back at the top of the village, near The Old Spring ❺ and Ognistra Taverna ❻.

Ahead, you can clearly see the pink belfry of Iakovos, Persis.

SIDE VIEW OF IAKOVOS, PERSIS

ΠΛΑΓΙΑ ΟΨΗ ΤΟΥ ΑΓΙΟΥ ΙΑΚΩΒΟΥ ΤΟΥ ΠΕΡΣΗ

You are now back at the top of the village, where your walk began. From here the options are...

1 **Meander back down** to one of the village tavernas, enjoy some home cooked food and quench your thirst.

2 **Explore a bit more** of the top of the village along the cobbled paths, farm tracks or little alleyways.

3 **Should you wish to** stay in Old Perithia there is a wonderful boutique bed & breakfast, the **Merchant's House**. Simply drop into **Ognistra** taverna to check availability.

4 **If you decide to look around more, or just want to wander around the village, then read on and check the map to see how close things are. If you're thinking of walking to Mt. Pantokrator, see pages 80-81.**

The Holy Church of Iakovos, Persis ❹ seen from the side, with its surrounding stone wall Η εκκλησία του Αγίου Ιακώβου του Πέρση, όπως φαίνεται από τα πλάγια, και το πέτρινο τείχος που την περιβάλλει.

Side view of Iakovos, Persis ❹ seen from the far side as you approach the point where the tour began Πλάγια όψη του Αγίου Ιακώβου του Πέρση, όπως φαίνεται από τα πλάγια καθώς πλησιάζετε το σημείο εκκίνησης της ξενάγησης.

HONEY ㉝

ΜΕΛΙ

Shortly, to your left down a small track as you head back towards Ognistra taverna is the home of Gerasimos and Stamatella. If you want to buy some of their honey, why not see if they are at home ㉝ **and** ask for **'Meli'** (honey in Greek).

The picture (below) shows the rows of beehives on the terraces that once accommodated corn and wheat, and now provide their bees with a perfect setting and a tranquil home.

THIS IS WHERE THE GUIDED TOUR ENDS

ΕΔΏ ΟΛΟΚΛΗΡΏΝΕΤΑΙ Η ΞΕΝΆΓΗΣΗ ΣΑΣ.

The beehives on the old corn and wheat terraces Τα μελίσσια στις παλιές καλλιέργειες σιτηρών

The cottages and beehives ㉝ of the oldest inhabitants of the village. Τα σπίτια και τα μελίσσια των παλιότερων κατοίκων του χωριού

> *"Gradually the magic of the island (Corfu) settled over us as gently and clingingly as pollen."*
>
> **Gerald Durrell 'My Family and Other Animals'**

RESTORATION AND RUINS

ΑΝΑΣΤΗΛΩΣΗ ΚΑΙ ΕΡΕΙΠΙΑ

The Holy Church of St. Nikolaos, Petra ㉙ Η εκκλησία του Αγίου Νικολάου της Πέτρας

The top of the village has been the catalyst for recent restorations and it's worth looking around to get a feel of how the village is now coming back to life.

Old Perithia was the first choice location for the film 'Captain Corelli's Mandolin'.

If you walk along a small track between the side of Ognistra and the back of The Merchant's House, between map points ❻ and ❾, you can explore still further and see a number of restored homes, and others in need of restoration. This includes a three-storey building (once owned by the Gerolimaios family) standing precariously close to the back of the goatherd's home. Beyond there, the ruins of a number of similarly imposing old houses, so you need to do a bit of exploring. With its historic setting, Old Perithia was the first choice location for the film 'Captain Corelli's Mandolin' however, disputes between the municipalities prevented it and a reconstruction was built in Cephalonia instead. **You can easily retrace your steps back to the top of the village.**

LEAVING OLD PERITHIA

ΑΦΗΝΟΝΤΑΣ ΤΗΝ ΠΑΛΙΑ ΠΕΡΙΘΕΙΑ

Finally, as you drive back out of the village, you may wish to stop at the slope on the right hand side of the road and walk up to **The Holy Church of Theotokos, The Virgin Mary** ❸ built between the 13th and 14th centuries. This is the church set up on the right-hand side as you leave the village. **Then, further along, on the left side** of the road, you will travel back past **The Church of St. Athanasios** ❷ nestling amongst the trees below. **You then pass back through gap in the rocks** ❶ that makes up the 'natural entrance', and now exit, from **Old Perithia** twisting down the mountains to the turquoise sea and sandy beaches below.

'There's something so beautiful, calming, peaceful, and spiritual about this place that each time you leave Old Perithia you may find yourself longing to return.'

Σε αυτό το μέρος κυριαρχεί μία έντονη αίσθηση ομορφιάς, ηρεμίας, γαλήνης και πνευματικότητας και κάθε φορά που αφήνεις την Παλιά Περίθεια σε διακατέχει μια έντονη επιθυμία να επιστρέψεις'

Leaving Old Perithia - Αφήνοντας την Παλιά Περίθεια

OPTIONAL WALK TO MOUNT PANTOKRATOR ㉞

ΕΝΑΛΛΑΚΤΙΚΗ ΔΙΑΔΡΟΜΗ ΠΡΟΣ ΤΟ ΟΡΟΣ ΠΑΝΤΟΚΡΑΤΟΡΑΣ

Unless you are well prepared to visit **Mount Pantokrator** ㉞ from Old Perithia, we recommend you enjoy the **circular tour of the village** and visit Pantokrator another time. If you want to walk from Old Perithia to Mount Pantokrator and back, then allow 1½ hours to get there and another 1½ hours to get back. The best time to walk is during the months of April, May and June when the temperatures are not so high and the flora and fauna are at their best.

There's a monastery at the top of **Mount Pantokrator** that was

Mount Pantokrator ㉞ looking past Iakovos, Persis (to the left) Παντοκράτορας

At 906m (2,972ft) Mount Pantokrator is the highest summit in Corfu. On clear days it's possible to see Italy, 130km (80 miles) away from the island.

built in 1347, around the same year as **Old Perithia** was established. When the original monastery, dedicated to Christ Pantokrator 'The Almighty' was built, the name was applied to the entire mountain. The original structures have been replaced a number of times over the centuries but were destroyed sometime around 1537. The current church on the site dates from around 1689, and the current façade was built during the 19th century.

Once known by the Venetians as Monte San Salvatore, the views from here are quite spectacular (ignoring the somewhat unorthodox communications towers). On a clear day you can see Italy, Albania and the island of Paxos in the south. There are some steps at the rear of the monastery that lead to a platform from where you get a good view of the interior and frescoes, most of which date back to the early 16th century.

Please Note (Παρακαλώ σημειώστε):
In early August there is the annual St. Saviour's Day celebration and it will be busy as there are pilgrimages to the monastery.

Mount Pantokrator from Corfu Town- Το όρος Παντοκράτορας από την πόλη της Κέρκυρας

Note: During the summer (as in other countries) there are snakes and scorpions around. It's unlikely that you will see any but, if you are walking it is wise to be on your guard. The grass snakes are harmless, however there are also a couple of venomous snakes and, although they are instinctively shy and will try to avoid you, do be aware and steer clear. It is advisable to wear good walking shoes and long trousers, stay on the path, take water and a mobile phone.

NOTES ON THE SURROUNDING NATURE AND WILDLIFE

ΦΥΣΗ ΚΑΙ ΑΓΡΙΑ ΠΑΝΙΔΑ

Photograph: Courtesy of Kolleen Ostgaard

Oak Trees, summer and winter. Βελανιδιές το καλοκαίρι και το χειμώνα

There are believed to be over 6,000 species of flowering plants in Greece. So you will not be surprised to learn that this ancient settlement, set in a mountainous landscape on the northern slopes of **Mount Pantokrator** ㉞ has a fusion of wild flowers with a plethora of herbs and shrubs. Old Perithia also has a great variety of trees (pine, cypress, oak, cherry, almond, walnut and fig) as well as a few olive groves and vines.

Historically, parts of Corfu were covered with natural oak forests. The Venetians mainly exploited these for construction and shipbuilding. Nevertheless, many oak trees can still be seen around the village to this day. The Venetians had also sought to make the island a major supplier of olive oil, used as a fuel for lamps. To this end they instigated the extensive planting of olive trees throughout the island.

However, there are many other types of trees in and around Old Perithia but only a few olive trees, as they were not best suited to the height of the village.

There are a number of tall elegant cypress trees (reminiscent of Tuscany) also known by the Greeks as **'Dachtila tou Theou'** which literally means, 'The fingers of God'. Rather appropriate for a village which name derives from the words **peri** and **theia** (surrounded by The Holy). You'll see plenty of these on your walk around. A few of these tall cypresses almost seem to 'frame' **The Holy Church of St. Nikolaos, Petra** ㉙ as you'll see when you glance back at the church from the upper path.

Others include; chestnut, citrus and holly

Nature and Wildlife engulf you as you travel up to Old Perithia and walk the paths around the village. Its wild beauty extends as far as the eye can see to the mountains and beyond.

oak trees, and of course, the elm trees in the village square.

The Venetians showed a special interest in agriculture, and encouraged the cultivation of olive trees, although at over 400m (420 - 480m) Old Perithia was not situated at an ideal height for olive groves so the villagers focussed on corn, wheat and livestock. Nevertheless, Corfu's countless olive trees still constitute its main agricultural product producing over 3% of the world's production.

Centuries ago, the number of trees in and around Perithia was estimated at approximately 100,000.

Fortunately some of these magnificent trees can still be seen to this day but the actual forest was thinned dramatically due to a number of complicated ownership issues and lack of official protection.

“In all of nature, in trees for instance, I see expression and soul…”
Vincent van Gogh 1882

Σε όλη τη φύση, στα δέντρα για παράδειγμα, βλέπω μορφές έκφρασης και ψυχής...'
Βίνσεντ βαν Γκογκ 1882

There is plenty of wildlife including snakes, geckos, lizards, dragonflies, butterflies and many birds, including birds of prey. There's even the odd tortoise! Nocturnal animals include bats, owls, toads, hedgehogs and, in the spring, mesmerising fireflies flicker in the night sky.

FLORA AND FAUNA

ΧΛΩΡΙΔΑ ΚΑΙ ΠΑΝΙΔΑ

The northern slopes are of a typical Mediterranean terrain with relatively mild winters. The humid, warm climate and the high degree of precipitations, combined with good soil conditions and geographic position of the island make this just the right place for a vast wealth and variety of flora and fauna.

Mid-February is blossom time for the first wild orchids, while in the beginning of Spring the area is full of chamomile. The countryside is at its best in April, May and June when the mountains are covered with a rich tapestry of colour, but remains beautiful throughout the year, as the countryside shows off its many different shades and blossoms throughout the seasons. There are wild cyclamen, sweet violets, hyacinths, iris and crocuses. Winter rain nourishes the entire mountainside and prepares it for its next annual display.

Hawks, eagles, peregrines, kestrels and buzzards may be seen hovering and darting through the air. There's also a bird's eye view of Old Perithia for visitors, seen from the path above the village, and on the way up to Mt. Pantokrator.

The old stone houses with their honey coloured roofs, the numerous wild flowers and the yellow, pink and white churches in the background blend to form a beautiful pallet

As you walk, listen out for the clanking of bells from the goats grazing on the mountainside and glance at the many beautiful butterflies as they flutter by.

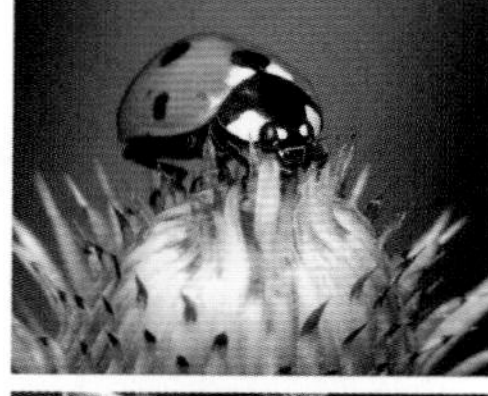

Old Perithia certainly justifies its dedication as 'an area of outstanding natural beauty'.

that is a painters' paradise. All of this, with the sea in the distance, creates a place where the sights and the smells of wild herbs will stimulate all of your senses.

Throughout the year you can find beautiful, and often rare, flowers in Old Perithia. These include; wild lavender, various heathers, oleanders, daisies, geraniums, marigolds, poppies, hyacinths, dwarf cyclamen, blue anemones, wild tulips, irises, bluebells, many purple and yellow crocuses, and in particular some extraordinary **orchids**.

There are around thirty to forty different varieties of orchids on the island.

The choice of herbs (i.e. oregano, mint and bay) and wild plants that can be found in Old Perithia are ideal for dishes such as **Horta or Tsigarelli.** Since the time of Hippocrates, the father of Greek medicine, the herbs and plants have long been famed for their medicinal properties.

Herbs and Medicine

Βότανα και ιατρική

The Ancient Greeks had an extensive knowledge of herbs and were aware of many herbal remedies. Commonly used herbs were; anise, black hellebore, cassia, root of (squirting cucumber), cumin, cyclamen root, frankincense, germander, honey, wild lettuce, myrrh, olive oil, opium poppy, parsnip and seseli. Many of these herbs and remedies are still used today.

INSPIRATION FOR EVERYONE

ΕΜΠΝΕΥΣΗ ΓΙΑ ΤΟΝ ΚΑΘΕΝΑ

Unsurprisingly, Old Perithia is an inspiring destination for many visitors. From **'off road' tours** to **day-trippers** and couples or **families** with (or without) children. The area is very popular with intrepid **walkers, lovers of flora and fauna (who say it's a botanist's haven), ornithologists, geologists, painters and art fans, architectural buffs, astronomers** and **photographers**. All of these come to visit the Old Village throughout the entire year to explore or capture this perfect display of nature's colours and creation.

The architectural and wild natural beauty of this settlement have also been the focus of a number of academic studies by scientists from Italian, French and German universities, visiting the village each year to study this unique 14th century legacy.

The Venetians had a profound influence on Corfu. Apart from the agricultural impact, their influence can be seen in architecture, education, art, music and entertainment, health systems, cuisine and in today's popular recipes.

The Corfu Trail

Οδηγός Κέρκυρας για περιπατητές

An island highlight, Old Perithia is indicative of the direction a small branch of Corfu's tourism industry is taking, a direction also underlined by the establishment of the Corfu Trail. Some of the abandoned houses in the village are being renovated, and more are for sale, awaiting a loving owner - an owner who prefers tradition and a peaceful setting to the brash modernism and clamour of the coastal resorts. Old Perithia is protected as a heritage village by the local council, and restoration work must be in keeping with the time-honoured building style. It is the most spectacular of the many villages which the Trail links, villages which offer an alternative to traditional, resort-based holidays. Here, local colour reigns over stereotyped entertainment.

Extract from an article on The Corfu Trail by its founder, Hilary Paipeti.

Food for Thought

Κουζίνα με άποψη

Natural ingredients can be found in abundance in Old Perithia, They are so organic and healthy that you can taste the goodness with every mouthful, from fresh crisp salads to succulent fruits and delicious honey drenched desserts.

Horta is a traditional cooked dish made from a variety of edible plants that grow in and around the village; dandelion, wild mustard, Neapolitan wild garlic, onion, endive and wild asparagus. The greens are boiled, covered with a little olive oil and lemon, and served as a side dish at the tavernas in the village. The spicy version of this is called tsigarelli.

Other locally sourced produce include some of the following; beef for pastitsada or sofrito, rabbit for stifado, home baked local feta cheese, spinach pie 'spanakopita' (below), sausages, tzatziki and of course Greek salad. For dessert, try a piece of delicious walnut pie soaked in syrup, known as karidopita.

OLD PERITHIA AND CORFU A SUCCINCT TIMELINE

ΠΑΛΙΑ ΠΕΡΙΘΕΙΑ |ΚΕΡΚΥΡΑ. ΣΥΝΤΟΜΟ ΧΡΟΝΟΛΟΓΙΟ

The Island of Corfu is steeped in history, in the timeline below we run through some key dates, highlighting events in Old Perithia (●) along the way.

According to mythology the name of **Corfu** (**Kerkyra** in Greek) is derived from the nymph **'Korkira'**.

Homer's 'Odyssey' mentions the island in one of the adventures of Ulysses. **'Poseidon, God of the Sea, fell in love with the nymph, kidnapped her and brought her to the island that then took her name.'**

Prehistoric Period
Archaeological excavations have proven that the island was inhabited since the **Paleolithic Era.** An important commercial centre inhabited by the **Phoenicians.**

8th century BC The island's first settlers were the **Eritreans** and soon after the Corinthians. Being the closest point in Greece to Italy, the island was the first to be invaded by the **Romans** in **229 BC**.

229BC-337AD Corfu was under Roman command. In 337AD when the Empire was split in to east and west, Corfu was incorporated in the east and subsequently became part of **Byzantium.**

337-1204 During the **Byzantine** period, the island was raided by **Genoese Pirates, Goths, Vandals, Saracens and Barbarians.** In 550 Corfu town (then **Corcyra**) was attacked by the Goths and was abandoned. A new town, from the Greek word 'Coryphia' (summit or peaks) was constructed. This being the origin of the islands more recent name. In **1081** Robert Guiscard the **Norman** and 'King of Sicily' took over the island, which was then liberated by the **Byzantine** Emperor Komninos c.**1149.** **From 1204 -1214** was a period of **Venetian** dominance. It lasted for only 10 years.

> *Poseidon, God of the Sea, fell in love with the nymph, kidnapped her and brought her to the island that then took her name.*
>
> **Homer's 'Odyssey' relates to the island in one of the adventures of Ulysses.**

1214 -1267 During this period in 1257 the Despotate of Epirus, an independent Greek state of Byzantine origin, took control of the island. In **1258** Corfu was captured by the Kingdom of Sicily. It was taken by the Angevins in 1267.

1267 - 1386 **The Angevin Period** saw the island split into four distinct areas. The period ended with the death of Charles III of Anjou, in 1386

In ● 1347 The settlement is established and the Perithiotes help with the building of the first monastery on Mount Pantokrator. The current church on the site dates from around 1689 with a 19th century façade. To give a European perspective at this time, the Black Death, the worst disease in recorded history, arrived in Europe and in England the following year in 1348.

● 1348 (approximately) **The Old Perithia Spring** is discovered by a village goat.

1386 **Corfu placed itself under the protection of Venice**, which in **1401** acquired formal sovereignty and ruled for four centuries. The **Greek Orthodox** religion and traditional customs survived.

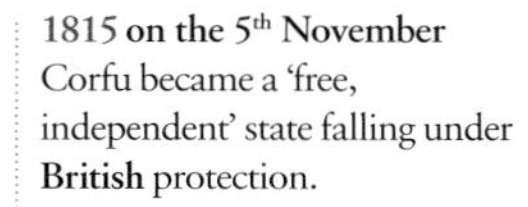

Kerkyra then remained in **Venetian** hands from 1402 until **1797**, though several times from 1431 assailed by Turkish naval and land forces and subjected to four notable sieges in 1537, 1571, 1573 and 1716.

1553 It is believed that **St. Spyridon** saved the island from famine, the first of many such beliefs involving the island's patron Saint.

1630 In this year on Palm Sunday, **St. Spyridon** drove off the plague from Corfu (and again in **1673**) dates that have been celebrated every year since.

● 1699 **The Mansion House** was built in Old Perithia for the wealthy **Skordilis** family. **Sieges continued** by the Turks, although in **1716 St. Spyridon** relieved the island of the siege of the Turkish army.

1797 The island was given up by Venice to Austria and the island then yielded to France.

1799 A Russo-Turkish force seized the island and the Septinsular Republic was established as a buffer state, including Corfu and a number of the other Ionian islands. Though nominally independent it was to all intents and purposes a Russian dominion.

1807 The Treaty of Tilsit returned Corfu to the French.

1815 on the 5th November Corfu became a 'free, independent' state falling under **British** protection.

● 1821 **Old Perithia was the capital** seat of the **Kassiopi** province until **WWII.** Then after the war each village became a separate municipality until c.1985 when it fell under the municipality of **Thinali.**

1835 The game of **cricket** was introduced to the Island, and continues to be played to the present day.

● 1863 **The Miracle of Old Perithia** when the children who were dying of a mysterious illness (probably diphtheria) returned to health after the entire village prayed to the Virgin Mary for a miracle. **Notably, that same year** on 23rd September came the **Resolution to unify the Ionian Islands with Greece.**

1864 **21st May Corfu becomes part of a United Greece** and the British Garrison departed by proclamation of the British Lord High Commissioner.

1912 **The Corfu Land Act.** After the union with Greece, Corfu's landed gentry gradually lost their wealth and status, and in 1912, the Land Act forced them to hand over much of their agricultural land to the local peasants who worked it.

● 1940 **The Old School was closed** and children were educated in the schools of New Perithia and elsewhere.

1939-1945 WWII. From 1940, **Greece was attacked by Germany.** On 6th April **1941** Corfu eventually surrendered. In ● 1945 **Old Perithia began to be deserted.** But in the following summers, the plagues of mosquitoes from Antinioti and other nearby coastal lagoons forced the inhabitants back to the village. By the **1960s Corfu developed as a tourist destination.**

● 1974 The village of **Old Perithia becomes all but abandoned** as the inhabitants return towards the coast where there are modern schools, shops and amenities.

● 1979 The settlement of **Old Perithia** was **decreed by the Greek Ministry of Culture**, to be listed as **a 'Designated Heritage Site'** and **'an Area of Outstanding Natural Beauty.'**

● Present Day **The village** tavernas and homes are being lovingly restored. This is in accordance with the public protection order to help ensure the preservation of this historic village, and in an effort to restore its once thriving local community.

MAIN FESTIVALS AND CALENDAR OF EVENTS

ΕΟΡΤΟΛΟΓΙΟ ΚΑΙ ΕΚΔΗΛΩΣΕΙΣ

1st January St. Basil's Day
New Years Day and the feast of Agios Vassilis celebrated with church services. Greek families cut 'vassilopita', a sweet bread with a coin inside which brings to its finder good luck for the year to come.

6th January Epihany
This is the feast of Agia Theofania, or 'Ta Fota' celebrating the day when the 'kalikatzari' (hobgoblins that appear during the period of Christmas) are banished back to the netherworld by the church's rites. On this day a cross is thrown into the sea off Mandraki (beneath the Old Fortress) for divers to 'rescue' and one lucky swimmer wins goodwill (and some money!)

End of February-early March Carnival Season
The Carnival is called 'Apokries' in Greek and is expressed by three weeks of feasting and dancing. Important Carnival Parades take place in Corfu with wonderful parties. The Carnival takes place three weeks before Lent and the exact dates vary depending on Easter. The Monday after the Carnival is known as Clean Monday and marks the first day of Lent.

March 25th Independence Day
The Greeks celebrate the day they declared the Revolutionary War against the Turks, on March 25th, 1821.

Palm Sunday St. Spyridon's Day
The remains of St. Spyridon are carried, in procession, around Corfu town to commemorate the miraculous deliverance of the island from a deadly plague.

Holy Week
Throughout Corfu this is characterised by its church services, fasting, and the anticipation of the Resurrection. This is a great

time to visit the countryside as the season changes from Winter to Spring.

Easter (dates vary)
Easter is the most important festival of the Greek Orthodox Church. It starts seven weeks before Easter Sunday.

Good Friday
A special celebration takes place. This festival is huge and of great importance, and Corfu is certainly the most famous for its wonderful array of celebrations.

Good Saturday
The Procession of St. Spyridon to commemorate the relief of the island from famine, and this is the oldest of the four processions. At 11am, the Pot Throwing ceremony takes place along the Liston Esplanade which symbolizes the 'first Resurrection' of Christ. In the evening there are church services and music from the philharmonic orchestras. At midnight a symphony of fireworks explode in the skies above to create a beautiful spectacle.

Easter Day
After midnight, families and friends eat and drink as the Resurrection is celebrated and the Lenten fast is broken. Further processions and parades take place in the morning, and there's a lamb spit roast for a truly delicious Easter lunch.

1st May Labour Day
This feast is called Protomagia (meaning first day of May) and this is a holiday when people traditionally go to the countryside for a picnic.

21st May Ionian Day
Enosis (Union with Greece). An annual procession in Corfu town and celebrations in various villages.

June (date varies) Whit Monday
Feasts to the honour of God the Holy Spirit.

Last Sunday in July
The Procession takes place for 'The Miracle' of The Virgin Mary in Old Perithia. It starts at Iakovos, Persis or St. Nikolaos, Petra (alternating each year) and proceeds around all of the churches of the village.

6th August Feast of the Transfiguration of Christ
On this day, and during the preceding week, there are pilgrimages to the monastery at Mount Pantokrator.

11th August St. Spyridon's Day
The Procession and festivals to commemorate the intervention of St. Spyridon during the Turkish invasion in 1716 when a terrible storm broke out as the invading force tried to besiege Corfu, causing their retreat.

15th August Assumption of the Virgin Mary
A National Holiday with festivals in many Corfiot villages

28th October 'Ochi Day'
This day is characterised by military parades. It is called 'Ochi Day' (No Day) to commemorate the negative

answer by the Greeks when the Italians asked them to surrender during World War II, on October 28th, 1940.

1st Sunday in November
The Procession of St. Spyridon for saving Corfu from a deadly plague, which visited the island twice in the 17th century.

12th December St. Spyridon's Day
Local Holiday with a day long festival in Corfu Town.

24th December
Carol singing, hymns and celebrations leading up to Christmas Day.

25th December
Christmas Day and holiday on the 26th too.

GETTING TO OLD PERITHIA

ΠΩΣ ΘΑ ΦΘΑΣΕΤΕ ΣΤΗΝ ΠΑΛΙΑ ΠΕΡΙΘΕΙΑ

The village of Old Perithia is approximately 50km (1 hour drive) from Corfu Town along the north east coastal road. The turn off is between Kassiopi and Acharavi.

Driving on the coastal road pass Kassiopi and after about 5-6km keep your eyes peeled. The turning is signposted Loutsa|Peritheia. On your left, look out for the peach coloured entrance wall (below) and on the right, a delicious ice-cream parlour, with the distinct cone on the roof. **This is where you turn up the road towards Old Perithia!**

Keep going for a very short while and then follow the sign (below) taking the left road to 'Old Village of Perithia.'

Following the road, quite soon there's a fork in the road. Turn to the left (do not go straight on) at the fork and keep following the signs to Loutses and Old Peritheia (below, then go through Loutses).

Continue through the village and along the winding road for about 3km until you pass through Loutses.
Soon afterwards you'll see two signs ahead Anapaftiria and Ano Perithia (Upper Perithia). Continue straight towards Ano Perithia! (not Anapaftiria.)

At this point (if you haven't already), open your windows and enjoy the natural perfume of scents and smells that emit from the numerous flowers, trees and herbs that carpet the mountains around you.
Continue on the now narrow and winding roads (drive carefully) and the road will turn to tarmac, winding along until you see the sign below just before a hair pin bend.

Stay on the main road (do not go up the track ahead!) Soon you can see Pantokrator ahead as you pass by an old stone stables to the right.
You will then pass the cut away hill next to a small icon as shown above.

By now you are very close to Old Perithia.
From here the road starts to trail down and you'll see the village ahead of you and, to the left, the pink façade of The Holy Church of Saint Iakovos, Persis ❹.

Parking Πάρκινγκ
Please park carefully and considerately, as far back from the start of the main village as possible, to help retain the natural view of the church, historic houses and restored taverna as you enter the village. Also, the local goatherd and his wife often need to cross the road and have access to drive or walk in and out of the village (with their goats or sheep) so please don't block the roads and pathways.

Disclaimers and Copyright

Merchant's House Publishing
The Merchant's House
Old Perithia
49081 CORFU
Greece
e. editor@old-perithia.com

Additional information, acknowledgements, copyrights and research material

Thanks to:
Nikos Chirdaris. Spiros Zervopoulos (architectural drawings) and for use of his and Peppi's wonderful bookshop in Corfu town. Mihalis Kokkalis. Loukas Skordilis. Dimos Papadatos. Arturo, Wilma and Dimitri Zervos. The former inhabitants of Old Perithia who helped us with their time, knowledge and memories.

Extracts taken from:
Libro d'Oro. 'The History of the island of Corfu' by H Jervis-White Jervis published in 1852. Noble Houses of Corfu, by Despina Paisidou. Class formation in the Ionian Islands during the period of British rule, 1814-1864 by Dr Sakis Gekas.

Quotes and extracts from:
Prospero's Cell by Lawrence Durrell and Birds, Beasts and other Relatives by Gerald Durrell. Article on The Corfu Trail written by its founder Hilary Paipeti. Quote from Daniel Rozensztroch, 'Greek Style'.

Written and researched by:
The guide was written, researched and is published by Mark Hendriksen. Editorial, photography*, map and walking tour written and devised by Mark Hendriksen.

Editorial assistance, sub editing and proof read:
James Marsh of b3 and Saskia Bosch.

Map and Illustrations:
Mark Hendriksen, Peter Barrell and Spiros Zervopoulos.

Photography:
With the exception of black and white pictures on p2, 8 ,9 ,11, 24, 25, 31, 57, 64, 69 & 73 kindly provided by Mihalis Kokkalis. 'The Vigla', window on Perithia and inside the house with sundial (2004) by Alkistis Prepis. Cretan Lion from Wilma & Dimitri Zervos. **i-stock images as follows:** contents p3, orchid p15, coffee setting p17, Greek dancing p38-39, olive press p44, olive branch p57, chicken p75, bee p77, almonds p82, figs, butterfly and tortoise p83, orchid, ladybird and eagle p85, spinach pie p87, cricketer p89, pots p90, church candles & fireworks p91. 'Winter oak leaves' by Kolleen Ostgaard.

First Edition 2010.
ISBN: 978-0-9565443-0-8

Design: Peter Barrell.

Translations
Thanks to: Nikos Chirdaris, Spiros Zervopoulos, Naya Hadzipani, Saskia Bosch and Christos Angelis.

Thanks
With thanks to: EOT and the Archaeological Department of Corfu for their support. We hope that Old Perithia will gradually be fully restored and become a vibrant community once again. May the village's restoration and status as a 'Heritage Site and Area of Outstanding Natural Beauty' encourage future generations to visit and inspire them to ensure this rather special part of Corfiot history remains alive.

Dedications
Thank you to Saskia my amazing and multi-talented wife, and to Christiaan and Gemma with love from their Dad. To our family and friends, and especially to Nikos Chirdaris, Spiros Zervopoulos, Kostas and Natalia Vardouniotis, and George Agious for their belief and support that has, and continues to be, invaluable.

Comments and Suggestions
We'd love to hear your comments and suggestions. Also, on any details that you may wish to add, or advise us on, so we may continually strive to improve the content and information provided in the guide. **Please email the editor directly**
editor@old-perithia.com